LIVING
AT THE
SPEED OF LIFE

Staying in Control in a World Gone Bonkers!

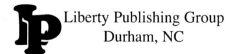

Cher Holton, Ph.D.

Artwork by Robert Belcher
Cover Design by Joe Balint

Liberty Publishing Group
Durham, NC

This publication is designed to provide accurate and authoritative
information in regard to the subject matter covered. It is sold with the
understanding that the publisher is not engaged n rendering legal,
accounting, or other professional service. If legal advice or other
expert assistance is required, the services of a competent professional
person should be sought. From a Declaration of Principles jointly
adopted by a Committee of the American Bar Association and a
Committee of Publishers.

Library of Congress Cataloging-in-Publication Data

Holton, Cher, 1950-
        Living at the speed of life / Cher Holton
            p. cm.
        Includes bibliographical references.
        ISBN 978-1-893095-03-8
        1. Self-management   2. Simplicity 3. Time management
        II. Title

Printed in the United States of America

10   9   8   7   6   5   4   3   2   1

To Bil,
  *~ my marriage partner, my business partner and my dance
  partner ~ who makes it possible for me to live joyfully at
  the speed of life!*

• • • ACKNOWLEDGEMENTS • • •

This book could not have been written without the help of a lot of people, and this is the opportunity to express my gratitude. My wonderful husband, Bil, provided not only his phenomenal creativity, writing skill and editing talents to guide me through this process, but also gave immeasurable emotional support through the journey. Nancy Eubanks spent hours in typing this manuscript, and served as a sounding board for my ideas and my frustrations.

Robert Belcher created the marvelous artwork, demonstrating an amazing ability to translate the vague concepts of my brain into actual illustrations that make this book so meaningful and easy to use. Kathleen Lewis performed her wizardry in taking the manuscript and transforming it into a book format for the publisher. Joe Balint designed the cover art with his usual pizzazz and imagination.

My parents, Blaine and Marguerite Detrick, gave me the gift of a wonderful childhood, along with positive and spiritual roots that gave me wings to fly. And of course, this book would not have the strength of authenticity without all the clients who allowed me to share these techniques with them, and all the wonderful individuals who allowed me to use their stories, making everything in this book "tried and true," proven to work.

To all of you, I give my sincere and deep felt thanks!

TABLE OF CONTENTS

Physical Health

Mental Health

COMMUNICATING EFFECTIVELY

BUILDING A PROSPERITY CONSCIOUSNESS

CREATING JOY AND MEANING
IN YOUR WORK

• • • INTRODUCTION • • •

Do you feel frenzied, fragmented and frazzled? Is there too much change and not enough stability in your environment? Do you have too many responsibilities and not enough time or energy to enjoy life? Are you burned out, pulled in too many directions, exhausted by the effort of daily living? Are you seeking some sense of balance in your life? Do you feel like you're living in a world that has gone bonkers?

It may help you to know you're not alone! In my travels as a Corporate Impact Consultant and Professional Speaker, I am finding that people everywhere are feeling more frustrated and pressured than ever before. The responsibilities of daily life have become over-whelming; people are spending so much time and energy doing what *has* to be done, there never seems to be time and energy to do what they *want* to do.

The results of a recent research study conducted by Harvard University reported that U.S. wage earners are working the equivalent of an extra month of time on the job each year compared to a decade ago. Stress-related illnesses cost our nation $300 billion last year in medical costs and lost productivity. Fortune magazine reported that of 30,000 U.S. workers interviewed, 47% disliked or at best were ambivalent about the jobs they held. At a recent Inc. 500 conference in Norfolk, VA, the breakout session on banking drew 8 people, while the session right next door, Burnout on the Job, had standing room only, with the audience overflowing into the hallway outside.

The message is clear. We are working harder than ever, and enjoying it less. Time has become the currency of choice. In the past five years, 28% of Americans voluntarily made job changes that led to less income but more leisure time. You can almost literally hear people crying: "Stop the world! I want to get off!" We are struggling to keep up; we are trying to live at the speed of life!

The pressures of constant change, decreasing stability, increasing demands, and an upheaval in the values of the country are creating a sense of despair, anger and exhaustion that is beginning to take its toll. What I constantly hear is a plea for more "balance" in life . . . for the magic formula to bring some sense of sanity and peace back into daily living. But balance is no longer an option in today's fast-paced world, and magic formulas that promise it have come up far too short. This book will help you discover why that search for "balance" is creating such frustration.

Think about that word — Balance. The word itself implies an equal distribution among the varied aspects of your life. It forces you to try to designate the same amount of attention and energy to everything and everyone. It is unrealistic and unachievable, and only leads to more frustration and dissatisfaction. You'll never achieve balance. What you *can* achieve is HARMONY — a sense of inner peace resulting from focused choices of how much time and energy to give to all the important areas of your life.

Harmony comes from your ability to take responsibility in making wise choices to take control of your life in a world that is truly going bonkers. That is better than any magic formula that a life balance guru or fad-crazy book can promise. The power to live at the speed of life and stay in control in a world gone bonkers is within **you.** You are the one who has the power to make choices, to take control and keep it. This book gives you hundreds of powerful, positive choices you can make immediately, to regain control of your life and claim the inner peace and stability you deserve. This is an exciting time in which to be alive — but it requires a whole new way of living to be able to fully enjoy it. So get ready to make the choice — right now — to start your journey in living at the speed of life!

• • • HOW TO USE THIS BOOK • • •

This book gives you power — the power to create a sense of inner peace and harmony in your life, regardless of the chaos taking place around you. It is designed as a resource guide, to be used on an on-going basis rather than read from cover to cover. You can start anywhere, go anywhere, stop any time. And that's one of the new skills needed to live at the speed of life! We no longer have the luxury of time or energy to be able to read everything we *need* to read, let alone all the things we *want* to read. It is important to be able to grab the information we need on the run — and this book is designed to help you do just that.

Through my research and experience, I've discovered there are seven critical areas in life that we must manage to maintain a sense of sanity and control. When even one of these areas is attacked or thrown out of kilter, our life as a whole is affected. As I think about the interconnectedness of these seven major areas, I'm reminded of Muir's Law: *When we try to pick out anything by itself we find it hitched to everything else in the universe.* It is nearly impossible to extract any one area, and totally separate it from the other areas. That's why it's so important to have skills to deal with each these areas, and stay in harmony as you move through this crazy world.

The seven critical skill areas this book addresses are:
- Conquering Fear and Doubt
- Maintaining Good Physical and Mental Health
- Communicating Effectively
- Creating Joy and Meaning in Your Work
- Building a Prosperity Consciousness
- Enriching Interpersonal Relationships
- Transforming Time Robbers

Within the pages of this book, you will discover power through principles, techniques, inspirational messages, stories, and tested strategies. This is a book that is meant to be used. Dog-ear the pages; highlight meaningful passages; make notes to yourself in the margins. Start a journal to record your thoughts and exercises from this book, and to track the results you experience.

Here's the best part! Obviously, you will have a need for different types of things depending on the issues you are dealing with at any given time. To help you as you explore the ideas, concepts and "how-to" activities of the book, you'll see margin icons to indicate what kind of material is included in that section. The following guide will help you get the biggest return on your investment as you make this book your own.

- **Guiding Principle** — Solid, time-tested principles that provide direction and guidance as you seek to achieve inner peace, harmony and joy in your life.

- **Activity for Self Development** — Personal exercises designed to help you successfully discover your inner strength and power.

- **Inspirational Quote** — My favorite quotes that can provide inspiration or strength as you take your developmental journey.

- **Question/Answer Segment** — Some of the most-often-asked questions from my workshops and one-on-one coaching sessions, along with my answers.

- **Research** — Results of research that support the principles, ideas and recommendations in this book.

- **For Your Tool Kit** — Practical techniques that you can implement immediately to help you live successfully at the speed of life!

- **Stories/Illustrations/Real Life Examples** — Specific examples to make the content of this book real for you.

- **Clipped from the News** — Related articles that appeared in either a newspaper or magazine.

The search for self-development and inner peace is an on-going journey, filled with huge jumps forward as well as stumbling blocks and detours. It is easy to give up, or worse yet, never begin. Many folks think about the journey, plan it, talk about it, but never take that first step. I have a quote on my desk that continues to inspire me as I take each next step toward my own evolvement. May it be an inspiration to you as you begin your journey through this book, and discover your own power to live at the speed of life, and stay in control in a world gone bonkers:

Leap, and the net will appear — or

I will discover I have wings to fly!

CONQUERING FEAR
AND DOUBT

CONQUERING FEAR AND DOUBT —
SNEAK PEEK

Fear immobilizes. When you experience fear or doubt, you feel paralyzed - emotionally and physically, and you are unable to move ahead with whatever it is you want to do. Fear and Doubt are the two biggest enemies we face in our journey through life. Therefore, it is essential that we have skills in our tool kit to recognize these dragons when we meet them, and slay them so we can move on to our next leap forward.

Some fear is normal — it is a natural companion of growth. And some fear is healthy, for it can warn you of danger or indicate that you need more information or training. For example, if friends want you to learn to ski by starting on the high slopes, your fear is actually a warning signal that says there is a better, safer way to start.

In this chapter, I'm talking about paralyzing fears that keep you from stretching yourself to your fullest limits. For example, perhaps you suffer from the #1 fear in America. Honest...according to research presented in *The Book of Lists*, the #1 fear of Americans is fear of public speaking. Anyone out there suffer from it? You're not alone. It ranks *above* fear of death — which tells me people would rather *die* than get up in front of an audience to speak!

You know how that kind of fear feels. Think back to a time when you had to give a speech in front of a big crowd, or were asked to perform some feat without the confidence in your ability. Remember the fast, shallow breathing? The butterflies in your stomach? The cold sweat? The shakes and dry mouth? These physical symptoms are easily recognizable. But the emotional masks that fear wears are less obvious, more subtle, easier to misdiagnose, and capable of sabotaging our joy and personal growth.

Let's take a look at some of the masks that FEAR can wear. For example, have you ever experienced the following?

- *An overwhelming desire to sleep.* Your body will use sleep as an excuse for not taking action. I talked about this in one of my seminars, and one of my participants - a marine - shared how on his first parachute expedition, the whole platoon was in the plane, and as soon as they took off, almost all of them fell asleep. He admitted they were scared to death! If you are experiencing an unusual drop in energy, the first thing to do is ask yourself if you are facing something you fear.

- *A sudden focus on trivial matters.* Often the mind uses a "Substitution Strategy" to mask fear. My fear of rejection when I need to make cold calls often masquerades as a need to reorganize my file cards before making those calls.

- *Renewed interest in some long-range, currently out-of-reach goal.* Dreaming of the future keeps your mind off the current issue you're avoiding, and very often leads to the next mask of fear.

- *Feelings of inadequacy.* We envision our inability to achieve some outrageous goal, then belittle ourselves, saying "What's the use? I'll never be able to do that." And so ... we never even attempt it.

It is very normal to experience fear and doubt, but don't let them paralyze you. Use the information in this powerful chapter to arm yourself against the immobilizing impact of fear and doubt. When you move through fear and doubt, you experience an exhilaration and zest for living that is unbelievable, and your power center is strengthened. Each experience you have with these deadly dragons empowers you to face life at a whole new level, achieving the inner peace and joy you deserve.

THE LESSON OF THE ZIP-LINE

One of the most powerful lessons I've ever learned — one that has truly empowered me against all kinds of self-defeating fears — took place on an Outdoor Challenge Course. I was there because Bil, my risk-taking husband, had *dragged* me to it kicking and screaming. He said: "It will be so much fun! Trust me!" Ever heard those words before?

If you've never had the opportunity of participating in one of these events, let me describe it. We went out in the woods for two days with a team and were challenged to accomplish a variety of initiatives. For example, we did trust-falls off 6-foot high posts; negotiated a complicated maze — blindfolded; scaled over a 12-foot wall with no resources other than our team. It was great fun, and I told Bil that first night that he was right, it was so exhilarating! He looked at me excitedly and said, "Just wait! Tomorrow will be even better — Trust me!" That should have warned me.

The second day was high events, which meant we were anywhere from 25 feet to 90 feet off the ground — walking on wires across a gorge; climbing poles and walking over tree-limb balance beams. In case you're wondering, I can assure you you're very safe — you have plenty of safety gear, and two belayers — safety is critical, and guaranteed. You know you're safe in your logical mind — but somewhere between your mind and your heart, you forget — and FEAR creeps in.

The final event of the day was the ZIP-line, which consists of a cable stretching through the trees at a height of about 90 feet. I want to be sure you comprehend the height of this cable. Imagine that you walk into a hotel, get into the elevator and go up to the ninth floor. You get out, enter a room and go out onto the balcony. As you lean over the balcony rail, in that room on the ninth floor, you are looking down from about ninety feet. Now, take away the hotel room behind you. Take away the balcony railing. There you are, on that zip-line platform, ninety feet high! Get the feeling?

As you stand on that little platform about 90 feet up in the air, the course facilitator hooks you up to the ZIP-line, you walk to the edge of the platform, look out into nothingness, and guess what they tell you to do? Jump! It goes against everything you've ever been taught. But when you jump, you zip on the cable through the woods, at about 30 miles per hour for 600 yards. It is really exhilarating... everyone said.

I did *not* want to do it! So I did what any sane, normal person would do — I waited 'til last! The longer I watched, the more scared I became. My stomach churned — my knees were weak. I'm thinking: "Another fine mess Bil has gotten me into!"

Finally, there was no one left...it was my turn and there was no way out. So I took a deep breath and began. I made it to the 90-foot platform — which for me was a major accomplishment. I'd like you to join me in your imagination — we're 90 feet up, standing on a tiny, little platform, with nothing around us. Can you feel it? Our team is down below — they look about 2 feet tall. They're all cheering "You can do it! You can do it!" We're looking out at the tops of trees, and there's a light breeze today. Can you feel us swaying with the breeze?

The course administrator got me all hooked up and said, *"OK, Cher, you're ready, Jump!"*

I said, *"Wrong!"* I could not move. [Remember — Fear paralyzes!] My feet felt glued to the platform — my palms were sweaty — I couldn't breathe. I'd *never* experienced such panic.

Now I have to admit that I really was not in the mood to do this. I'd been in the woods for two days — my hair was a mess, and I'd broken a fingernail on a prior event!

And now they expected me to jump!

I pointed to a tree about 5 feet away from me and said, *"If I jump, I know I'm going to hit that tree!"*

The course administrator tried a logical approach. She said, *"Cher, you've just watched eleven of your teammates go down this zipline. Now, think back. Did any of them hit that tree?"*

I had to admit they hadn't. She continued. *"Cher, look at the tree. Do you think it's going to move?"* As I shook my head, she ended by saying, *"No one has ever hit that tree! Trust me!"*

My team was on the ground, encouraging me. Finally they started yelling, *"Push her! Push her!"* The message was clear: People can only support you in your fear for so long!

One of the things I've noticed about fear is that once you give in to one fear, other fears kick in and join it. So now, in addition to my fear of heights, I was experiencing fear of looking silly in front of my teammates, fear of rejection, fear of failure, and maybe fear of death!

Finally, out of absolute need to perform in front of my peers, I decided to grit my teeth, close my eyes, take a deep breath and jump! I s c r e a m e d the whole way down — but let me tell you that when I got to the end, I felt great! I was exhilarated! I was charged! I looked back up from where I'd jumped, and shouted *"WOW! I want to do that again!"*

My reasoning was that the first time I was too afraid to enjoy it, and I wanted to do it again for fun. So we did. Bil and I went through the weekend a second time, I got to the final event — up on that 90-foot zip-line platform, and guess what? I was more scared the second time than I was the first time. I couldn't believe it. Have you ever been scared down to your toenails? So scared you felt sick on your stomach? That was me! My knees were like jelly…

I was hyperventilating…I could not jump. I looked at the course administrator (who was probably thinking: *here we go again — the wimp!*) and asked, *"Why am I afraid? I know my equipment is safe; I know I have two belayers supporting me; I know I'm not going to hit that tree; the amazing thing is I even know when I get to the end, I'll feel absolutely wonderful! So why am I so afraid?"*

Her response was the most powerful message about fear I've ever heard. She looked me straight in the eyes and said, *"Cher, the important thing is not that you get over your fear, because you may never get over this particular fear. The important thing is to DO IT ANYWAY! Empower yourself over your fear, so you know you're stronger than it is."*

And, I am pleased to inform you that I closed my eyes, took a deep breath, and I jumped… s c r e a m i n g again all the way down! But when I got to the end that time, I knew I truly could do anything I set my mind to, regardless of what fear I might encounter.

How has this helped me? In my job, one of the things I have to do is make cold calls to generate business. I do not like doing it, because I have a fear of rejection. [Can you relate?] And so, I can find all kinds of things to do instead of making those calls: clean out a file cabinet; work on proposals, develop a speech…all things that need to be done, certainly. But I was rationalizing to myself. [By the way, if you think about that word, *rationalize,* that's exactly what it is: **rational lies**. Lies that sound rational, but deep down, you know you're avoiding something more important.]

After the zip-line experience, I could look at my telephone and admit: "I don't want to make these calls. I've got a fear of rejection — but, it's OK — I'm going to DO IT ANYWAY!"And it's amazing how empowered I feel to overcome the fear that had paralyzed me.

TAKE OFF THAT FEAR MASK

You can recognize the mask of fear by acknowledging it, and calling it what it is. Ask yourself what you are afraid of. Then look at yourself in the mirror, acknowledge the fear, tell yourself it's okay to be afraid, then do it anyway!

DO IT ANYWAY!

The Zip-Line experience has become one of my "signature stories" which I often use in my speeches and workshops. During the break at one of my sessions, a woman came up to me and said, "Cher, you may not remember me, but I was in one of your workshops a few years ago, and you shared that same story about jumping from the Zip-Line. I never forgot it." She went on to tell me that about a year ago, her husband had been killed in a plane crash. She said, "Cher, there were so many times I was afraid, faced with things I didn't want to do. But I remembered your story, and I looked at myself in the mirror and said, 'It's O.K. to be afraid — but do it anyway!' And — I did it — and it felt g-o-o-o-o-d!"

WOW! What power there is in action! You don't have to jump off a 90-foot platform to empower yourself. All you have to do is think about yourself and ask: What kinds of fears am I experiencing that limit my growth? Fear of failure, fear of rejection, fear of looking dumb, fear of asking questions, fear of being wrong, fear of change, fear of the unknown? Whatever fears may be a part of your script, confront them now. Recognize the fear — acknowledge it — then, do it ANYWAY!

SMALL CHANGE = POWERFUL RESULT

What images, feelings, thoughts, or memories come to your mind when you hear the word "scared?" Take a few moments to really focus on the word "scared," and get in touch with what that word evokes within you.

Now focus on the word "sacred." What images, feelings, thoughts or memories come to your mind when you hear the word "sacred?" Take a few moments, and get in touch with what that word evokes within you.

I guarantee you have powerfully different results with those two words, and yet they are almost exactly the same. Transposing two letters makes all the difference in the world. By making a tiny shift in your consciousness, you can transpose a scared moment into a sacred one.

SAY "HELLO ..."

When life throws you an experience that brings fear or doubt, simply say, "Hello! I wonder what your lesson is. I want to learn it quickly, so you don't have to come back and visit me again."

LISTEN TO YOUR BODY!

One of my most interesting — and meaningful — encounters with fear came through the experience of a Firewalk. During the preparation phase, prior to actually walking barefoot across hot coals (measured at almost 1300°), our leader helped us learn how to listen to our body as we faced our fears. If the body becomes tense, it may be sending us a warning that we are not mentally prepared for the task at hand — or that there is some danger we cannot see, but intuitively feel. If, however, our body feels relaxed and calm (albeit nervous), then we're prepared to forge ahead. It worked, and as I walked over the coals I felt such an exhilaration over my fear.

But how easily we forget! Several months later, I participated in an Outdoor Challenge Course (similar to the one of my Zip-Line fame). One of the events required us to stand on stumps of varying heights and distance, and jump off them toward a wooden pole, grabbing on to the

pole and hanging. If we missed the pole, we fell into the
extended arms of our teammates, who were poised and
ready to catch us.

As I stood on my selected stump, my body was
extremely tense — screaming at me not to jump. I failed to
listen. Silly me. I told myself it was unrealistic fear, I trusted my teammates, no problem. And so, I jumped. Well, I
missed the pole by a fraction of an inch, which would normally be no problem. However, I happen to have long
fingernails. As I stretched to grasp that bar, every nail
snapped off at the quick, creating lots of blood and pain.
What a way to relearn the lesson! Listen to your body.

*Our goal is not to get rid of those butterflies — just get
them to fly in formation!*

IF YOU COULD DO IT

I saw a poster once that read: *What would you attempt
to do if you knew you could not fail?* Now there's an interesting question. If you knew that your safety would be
guaranteed, what one or two adventure risks would you
like to experience? If you were assured of no repercus-
sions, what would you like to say — and to whom? If you
were promised no fallout, what job would you apply for;
what gamble would you take; what ways would you
stretch your envelope?

I can't promise you that you won't experience some
failure, but I can promise that you'll experience phenomenal excitement and growth when you approach life with
the gusto of confidence and success. Things may not turn
out the way you planned, but you will be a better person for
having taken the risk. So take a look at what you really would
like to accomplish, assess the risks versus the rewards, and
go for it. Take the approach that you will not fail, only grow.
You'll never achieve what you never go after.

Failure is not fatal. Failure should be our teacher, not *our undertaker. It should challenge us to new heights of accomplishments, not pull us to new depths of despair. From honest failure can come valuable experience.*

(William Arthur Ward)

THE ANECDOTE FOR FEAR

Fear knocked. Action answered. No one was there! The anecdote for fear is action. I read somewhere that you should do a thing you fear three times. Once to move through the fear you are feeling; a second time to focus on what it is you are doing; and a third time to decide whether or not you enjoy doing it.

The principle is: *When you experience fear, take action!*

WORRY JAR

Are you a chronic worrier? Do you waste enormous energy conjuring up problems with no conceivable solutions? Do you find yourself fretting or fuming over phantom events which haven't happened yet or probably never will occur? Do you worry because you haven't worried lately?

Worry is one of the most destructive and useless emotions we humans use to approach our problems. It drains our energy. It lowers our immune system. It programs us for failure. The Worry Jar is a simple technique designed to help you refocus your energy and take control over whatever is causing you so much grief.

Find a glass or plastic jar, coffee can or other small container that has a lid. Label it as your Worry Jar. Feel free to decorate the jar if your creative spirit moves you. Next, select a Designated Worry Time (DWT). This should be a specific time once a week (for example, Friday night at eight o'clock). Place your Worry Jar in a conspicuous place and then move on with life as normal.

Throughout the week, whenever you find yourself fretting over something — stop! Grab a piece of paper and pencil, record your worry, fold the slip of paper and drop it in your Worry Jar. Remind yourself to worry about it during your DWT . . . not now.

When it's time to worry according to your DWT plan, open the jar and read the worrisome entries. Some of the things you worried so loyally about are history and no longer relevant. That means you don't have to worry about them anymore. Gloat over them before you burn them in effigy or throw them in the trash. Some entries will still be pending issues, so worry about them for a few minutes. (Do you realize how tough it is to worry on demand? You'll probably find yourself laughing at your attempts to seriously worry!) Once you've worried sufficiently over your current problems, fold them again and redeposit them in the jar, where they'll be ready for next week's DWT.

During the next week add any new worries as they occur and wait until your DWT to open the jar again. Repeat this process for several weeks or longer, if you want, until you can control your penchant for worrying. Pretty soon you'll recognize how much energy you've been wasting on worry. Let's face it: either you can do something about the problem, in which case you should stop worrying and take action — or, you can't do anything about it, in which case it's a waste of time and energy to worry!

Worry has centrifugal force. It moves opportunities away from you. The gravity of chronic worry pushes people away from you and causes outposts of concerned on-lookers instead of communities of support. People carry around knapsacks of worry, despondency, apprehension, pessimism and depression. No wonder they're tired. Trade your knapsack for a jar.

It's hard to fight enemies who have outposts in your head.   *(Sally Kempton)*

ACRONYMS FOR GROWTH

Design Engineer: I experience fear and self-doubt all the time. These two emotions really keep me from doing a lot of things I'd love to do. Is there any little gimmick you can share that will help me look at them differently?

Cher: It's good you recognize that fear and doubt are blocking you from growth. This is the first step toward conquering them. Here's a little gimmick I use to help me get the right perspective when I sense fear or doubt are playing havoc with my brain. I turn them into acronyms: FEAR stands for: False Evidence Appearing Real. DOUBT stands for Delightful Opportunities Unbelievable But True. Those little statements remind me to look beyond outward appearances, recognize the opportunities, and take action.

Fear says: "Give me symbols or signs. Give me concrete evidence. Offer me guarantees. Give me something — anything — I can rely on. *Inner peace says:* Give me only this moment to take action, learn what I can and grow.

THE SUSPENDED FOOT

Working Mother of Three: Why do I doubt myself so much? I wish I were more sure of myself.

Cher: As long as you are human, you will have doubts and fears and frustrations. Everyone does. The key is to move ahead in spite of them. Let me offer you an analogy. When you climb a ladder, you lift your foot from one rung of the ladder in order to put it on the next higher rung. From the instant you raise your foot, there is nothing for that foot to stand on until you put it on the next rung. If you were to focus all of your attention and self-worth and confidence on the suspended foot, you would feel anxious and uncertain. But you're still holding on with your hands . . . And don't forget your other foot, which is firmly planted on the rung below. So you have more support when you face the unknown than you think…the two hands and one foot that are firmly attached to the ladder. In the real world education, talents, skills, attitude and friends are your anchors. The important thing to remember is, you're never alone…and you've got more inner strength and outside support than you think. Focus on those anchors, instead of your suspended foot!

A THOUGHT TO PONDER

Imagine how much more fulfilling and harmonious things would be if, instead of being guaranteed the pursuit of happiness, we were guaranteed the happiness of pursuit.

No one can predict to what great heights you can soar. Even you will not know until you spread your wings.

(Successories Plaque)

MASKS OF FEAR

Jealousy is one of the masks of fear. And so is gossip. And so are slights and character assassinations and withholding helpful information and denying love and manufacturing hate and perpetuating prejudice. These are the fears which say *someone else seems to be getting what is rightfully mine and I'm too frightened to ask for it.*

Self-doubt can snipe at us and lure us into self-sabotage. A common form of this sabotage is substituting the expression "I can't" for legitimate action.

(Bil Holton)

AM I REALLY LAZY?

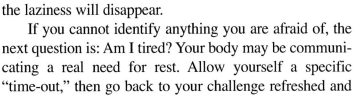

Sometimes what seems to be laziness isn't laziness at all, but fear — fear of failure, fear of change, fear of the unknown. When you think you are lazy, take a step back and ask yourself this question: What am I afraid of? The answer may surprise you! Unacknowledged fear is an absolute energy drainer. Focus on handling the fear, and the laziness will disappear.

If you cannot identify anything you are afraid of, the next question is: Am I tired? Your body may be communicating a real need for rest. Allow yourself a specific "time-out," then go back to your challenge refreshed and ready for action.

CHANGE YOUR MIND

Maintenance Supervisor: Cher, you said we can invent our future by imagining it. Do you really believe that or is that something all you motivational speakers say?

Cher: Do I detect a tinge of cynicism in that otherwise confident manner of yours?

Maintenance Supervisor: A little guardedness, perhaps. I *want* to believe I can substantially change my future.

Cher: You have the power today, in the present moment, right now, this very minute, to change any of your limiting beliefs or attitudes and to engineer the future of your choosing. As you change your mind, you change your experience. When you change your experience, you change your present. When you change your present, you invent your future.

Doubts, whether you whisper them or make them public, are like shadows which lurk in the dark, making the wary traveler afraid to pass.

(Bil Holton)

OPTIMISM YIELDS SUCCESS

It has been proven by Martin Seligman (University of Pennsylvania) that optimists are more successful than equally talented pessimists in business, education, sports and politics. For Metropolitan Life he developed a test to sort optimistic from pessimistic salespeople. The optimists outsold pessimists by 20% the first year, and by 50% the following year.

There is a vitality, a life force, an energy, a quickening, that is translated through you into action, and because there is only one of you in all time, this expression is unique. And if you block it, it will never exist through any other medium and will be lost.

(Martha Graham)

No one can persuade another to change. Each of us guards a gate of change that can only be opened from the inside. We cannot open the gate of another, either by argument or by emotional appeal.

(Marilyn Ferguson)

RETAILING SUFFERING

Employee Benefits Counselor: People tell me about their trials and tribulations all day. And some of them are pretty bad off. But all of them have one attitude in common - they don't seem to want to move to solutions. Why do people seem to brag about their suffering instead of moving beyond it?

Cher: That's what is so sad. People wear pain and suffering like a badge of honor, retailing it wherever they go. I don't believe we were put here to suffer. We were put here to learn…and not take ourselves too seriously…and to ease other people's burdens…and to have fun whenever we can.

Alleviating people's suffering is your area of expertise, but I'll give you my spin on it. Bragging about problems and suffering is one of the masks of fear — for example, a focus on suffering may be manifestation of fear of taking responsibility for one's health . . . or fear of assuming control without the help of others. Wanting attention, but fearing affection. Fear of being alone. Fear of not living up to others' expectations.

It's a cry for help. So those of us who are healthy and able need to calm the fears of those who aren't. No one should have to suffer. Mending their fragile egos takes time and patience and compassion. And by the way, they have to *want* to mend it! You can't "fix" someone who doesn't realize they're "broke!"

When in doubt, doubt doubt.

(Bil Holton)

WORST/BEST FANTASY

The Worst/Best Fantasy is a great technique to help you move through your fear and decide what action to take. It challenges you to take a stand — step out and make a decision, then go for it with confidence. Here's how it works.

Clearly describe the action you want to take, but feel powerless to do. It could be anything. For example, I've seen managers struggle with hiring, disciplining or firing an employee; a salesperson hesitate to make the necessary cold calls; a service rep fail to handle a complaint appropriately; an individual refuse to ask for help when it is really needed; etc.

Once you've identified the issue and selected the appropriate action you want to take, close your eyes and see yourself doing it. Ask yourself, "As I do this, what is the worst that could happen?" Plunge headlong into the fantasy and visualize all the things that could possibly go wrong. Take mental notes.

Relax for a moment. Then ask yourself, "As I do this, what is the Best that could happen?" Again, let yourself really fantasize. And again, take mental notes.

Now it's time for a reality check. Look at your "Worst" fantasy and ask yourself: "What are the chances that any of this will happen? If it did, how could I handle it?" Do the same for your "Best" fantasy.

It's often amazing when you logically analyze your fear how much of it is probably not going to occur, and how much positive pay-off there could be. By confronting your worst fears, you are able to put them in perspective and deal with them. This encourages you to go for it.

Resolve to accept the worst, should it occur. Now you can stop worrying.

(Brian Tracy)

BE LIKE THE BIRD

Be like the bird
That pausing in her flight
While on boughs too slight,
Feels them give way
Beneath her, and yet sings,
Knowing she hath wings.

Victor Hugo

ADVANCE CONFIDENTLY

Henry David Thoreau offered excellent advice in terms of the value of approaching our dreams with confidence, in spite of doubt and fear. He suggests that if we advance confidently in the direction of our dreams, and endeavor to live the life which we have imagined, we will meet with a success unexpected in common hours. We will put some things behind, will pass an invisible boundary; new, universal, and more liberal laws will begin to establish themselves around and within us; or old laws will be expanded and interpreted in our favor in a more liberal sense, and we will live with license of a higher order of beings.

Create in you an irresistible energy, putting wings on your heart that will allow you to fly beyond all self-imposed limitations.

(Gerald Jampolsky)

If you doubt something enough, the mind will attract all kinds of reasons to support the disbelief . . . There are no guarantees. From the viewpoint of fear, none are strong enough. From the viewpoint of love, none are necessary.

(Emmanuel)

YOU ARE NOT YOUR DOUBTS

We all have our doubts. The important thing is not to let them paralyze you. For every part of you that doubts, there is also a part of you that is courageous...that knows you can succeed. If you recognize your own self doubt, you've taken an important step.

Okay, I see that confused look. You're thinking, "What step have I taken? I'm doubting!" Here's what's so interesting. You're admitting your doubt. Now, ask the

doubting you if it has a message for you or if there is
something it wants you to discover about yourself. Then
spend some time being quiet, listening to hear what
insights the doubting you has to share with the knowing
you. You are not your doubts. You are the self that experiences them, so doubts are only part of your negative
consciousness. Refuse to let the negative parts of you
control the whole.

 *Learn to get in touch with the silence within yourself and
know that everything in life has a purpose.*
(Elizabeth Kubler-Ross)

A FEAR LOG

 Keep a Fear Log. In a special notebook, make a note
of any experiences you have where fear is a factor.
Include the date, a thorough description of the event or
situation, and specific ways in which you reacted.
Identify physical characteristics (hyperventilating;
sweaty palms; rash on neck; etc.) as well as emotions
(tears; anger; uncontrollable laughter; etc.) and responses (refusal to participate; making excuses; doing
unimportant things; etc.) Use this log to recognize your
patterns, then select ways to overcome them.

 *We cannot escape fear. We can only transform it into a
companion that accompanies us on all our exciting
adventures . . . Take a risk a day — one small or bold
stroke that will make you feel great once you have done it*
(Susan Jeffers)

JUST FOR THE FUN OF IT!

 A great way to overcome fear and doubt is to do
something, knowing up front you won't be good at it.

The point is to move through the fear of looking silly and the doubt in your ability by putting yourself in a position to willingly experience those feelings.

We miss out on a lot of joy in life because we won't try things we know we don't do well. Choose something you've always wanted to do, but were afraid to try . . . or something that a friend or significant other wants you to do, but you've resisted because you'd never done it before. Then, do it — just for the fun of it! Make it okay to be "unperfect." Laugh a lot, and fully experience the growth of stretching beyond your comfort zone. And if you find you're really enjoying the activity, move on to the "Start Small" Tool Kit idea.

THE FUN OF FEAR

Allow yourself the luxury of trying things you don't think you can do. Give yourself permission to look silly, make a fool out of yourself, admit what you don't know, enjoy the process. You will burst out of your comfort zone and experience a whole new level of energy and growth.

THE POWER OF FEAR

Billy Crystal admitted in an interview that he was terrified (yes, terrified!) whenever he stood in front of an audience. But he went on to share what I believe is one of the most powerful statements there is about fear. He said, "Fear is good. It gives you the edge!" We must learn to transform the fear we are feeling into energy to push us beyond the norm, to unbelievable heights of excellence.

To live a creative life, we must lose our fear of being wrong.

(Joseph Chilton Pearce)

THE WATER SKIING LESSON

So often, our fear of not doing something perfectly keeps us from experiencing the fun of exploration. I asked myself what messages I'd shared with myself about things I wasn't good at. One came into my mind immediately: I'm not athletic. So I decided to act on my own advice. I had an opportunity to go boating with friends, who urged me to try water skiing. Normally I would decline (Remember, I don't see myself as athletic), but I decided to give it a shot. It was hilarious — especially putting the skis on! I was exhausted before I ever reached the point of getting up! And, I took several falls as I made my attempts. I've never laughed so much in my life! And because I laughed at myself, it gave everyone else permission to laugh, too, as they gave much-needed advice. Guess what? I did it! And it was fun! I'll never ski at Cypress Gardens, but no one said I had to. You don't have to be perfect at everything you do. But my *fear of looking silly* kept me from experiencing things for many years.

START SMALL

Much of our self doubt comes from setting expectations that are unrealistic for ourselves. For example, you'd love to be a writer, but expect your first book to be like John Grisham or Tom Clancy. You work at a corporation and expect to be a vice president immediately. As a personal example, I love ballroom dancing, but got really frustrated by comparing myself to my instructor, who'd been dancing since she was three and had just won a National Championship. Talk about setting myself up for failure!

Here's a way to nip the self-doubt/over-expectation issue in the bud. Give yourself permission to do something badly at first, so you can learn to do it well. Experience small steps in your skill development, and compare yourself only with YOU, not the best in the field. Face your self-doubt by establishing realistic expectations at each level of your skill development.

I don't try to dance better than anyone else, only better than myself.

(M. Baryshnikov)

TEN SECRETS TO OVERCOME FEAR OF PUBLIC SPEAKING

Since Fear of Public Speaking is a major issue, and since so many professionals are faced with the need to do it, I thought I'd share my *Ten Best Tips* to help you conquer that fear, and turn it into an asset.

1. Rehearse your presentation out loud numerous times before you give it. Practice, practice, practice. Rehearsal leads to "muscle memory." When your mind forgets, the body takes over, and carries you through to your next segment.

2. Don't let 'em see you sweat. If during your presentation you hear your voice tremble or feel uncomfortable in any way (moist palms, dry mouth, nausea, shortness of breath) remember this: Generally, audiences will not notice a speaker's apprehensions if the speaker doesn't draw attention to them. They can't see what's going on inside! Take a few sips of water to relax your vocal muscles.

3. Memorize your outline, not your presentation. Internalize your speech so you'll deliver it naturally, with built-in flexibility. When you memorize, it forces you to do it exactly the same each time. If you forget a word, you're stuck. But if you know the general concept of your message, the right words will come. And by the way, it's perfectly okay to use notes. Keep them brief, with key points and words to trigger your memory.

4. Don't allow little mistakes to throw you off course. If you stumble, make an occasional grammatical error, mispronounce a word, or get tangled up on a phrase — don't focus on the mistake. Keep focused on the message you're communicating. Most listeners will not even notice your misfires — so fake it 'til you make it.

5. Use familiar illustrations, stories and humor to make your points. Unrehearsed and untried content adds unnecessary pressure and stress. (This is especially true of jokes!)

6. Practice meditational breathing to center yourself immediately before your presentation. Breathe slowly and easily. Relax.

7. If you feel yourself hyperventilating, drink a few sips of water. Refrain from consuming coffee, tea or sodas immediately before you speak. Caffeine dries your mouth and throat.

8. Visualize your speaking success. Imagine, in your mind's eye, moving through your presentation with ease and confidence. See the audience responding to your presentation with enthusiasm, acceptance and appreciation. Remember: the audience *wants* you to be good! (Who wants to sit and listen to a bad speaker?)

9. Hunt for those friendly faces, and use them to boost your confidence. Use the *Eye Lock* technique (Look at one person at a time in different parts of the audience, focusing long enough to connect with them, but not so long it feels uncomfortable) to create the illusion of talking to one person at a time instead of feeling overwhelmed by the multitude. Appropriate eye contact is vital to ensuring your credibility and professional image.

10. Be yourself! Learn from other speakers, but adopt your own speaking style. You'll feel more comfortable and so will your appreciative audiences.

ENJOYING GOOD PHYSICAL AND MENTAL HEALTH

ENJOYING GOOD PHYSICAL AND
MENTAL HEALTH — SNEAK PEEK

If you have your health, everything else is icing! It's
true. All the money in the world will not buy you good
health. I have a friend who is the President of a major company. He has achieved much success and recognition in his
field, received tons of awards and amassed a substantial
fortune. He recently shared with me that he'd just been
diagnosed with inoperable cancer. As we cried together, he
tearfully confessed that he'd trade all his success and
material wealth for a clean bill of health in a heartbeat.

Why is it that we wait until catastrophe hits before we
take our health seriously? It's no coincidence that the treatment for nearly every disease includes a change in diet and
exercise habits. So why not make those changes *before* illness attacks?

And consider the impact of our mental health on our
ability to move joyfully through life. When fear, low self
esteem, negativity and depression take over, we lose our
ability to take control, try new things and triumph over
life's difficulties.

There is so much we *can* control in the area of health.
This chapter focuses on two critical dimensions: physical
health and mental health. There is research to support the
overwhelming correlation between the two, and their
impact on every other area in our life. So get serious about
you, and choose the techniques most appropriate for your
lifestyle. We'll begin with a focus on Physical Health, then
move into areas related to Positive Mental Health. Begin
now to take control of your life, gaining inner peace
through a healthy mind and body.

MMMM, AHHH, HHHH

You'll want to do this wonderful relaxation exercise in the privacy of your own special place. Anyone overhearing it may begin to wonder what on earth you're doing!

Get in a very comfortable position, sitting up. (If you lie down, you'll fall asleep. Trust me — I know!)

Take a few slow, deep inhalations to relax. Keep your shoulders relaxed and pressed down as you breathe in. Then say *mmmmmm* as you exhale. Make sure you keep saying *mmmmmmm* while you exhale fully. Intone the sounds of *m* for the next three to five minutes.

Now simply breathe easily and quietly for a few inhalations. The breaths should be slow and rhythmical. Inhale and exhale slowly for another three to five minutes.

Say *ahhhhhhhh* during your next exhalation, using your entire breath. Say *ahhhhhhhh* during several more breaths. Drop the *a* in *ah* when you exhale this time so that you pronounce only the *h* sound. Feel the *hhhhh* sound clearly at the back of your mouth. Say the *h* sound for several more exhalations.

Use the *m, ah,* and *h* sounds in this sequence when you feel tense, frustrated or just plain tired. You'll feel lighter and energized immediately.

THE POWER OF A DEEP BREATH

Think about what happens to you physiologically when you are under stress, pressure or emotional turmoil. Your breathing rate increases and becomes very short, your blood pressure sky rockets, and your mind is unable to focus clearly. By taking a deep breath, from your diaphragm, holding it, then slowly releasing it, your breathing slows down, your blood pressure lowers, and your mind becomes more rational.

As you release that deep breath, pay special attention to your neck and shoulders. You'll notice a weight falling away as you breathe away your tension.

THE IMAGE OF A LAKE

Imagine a lake that is rippled or choppy by a breeze. If you take notice, all the images that are reflected in that lake take on the rippled, unclear appearance. But if that lake becomes calm and smooth, so too are all the images smooth and clear.

Taking a deep breath does the same thing to your mind. When you are under stress, your mind is similar to that rippled lake. Everything reflecting into your consciousness takes on a fragmented, unclear appearance. Once you take that deep breath, your mind becomes like the calm lake. Suddenly everything is clearer, you can make wiser decisions and you feel more at peace.

MEDITATION

Gandhi was said to have meditated at least one hour a day, except when he was really busy. Then he would meditate for two hours.

LISTEN INSIDE-OUT

Close your eyes and listen. Sit motionless for five minutes. This will seem like an eternity, I promise! Listen intently, patiently, non-judgmentally. Become aware of all the sounds around you.

Keeping your eyes closed, cup your palms over your ears. Sit motionless for another five minutes. Listen to the energy of your own body. Listen to the humming of yourself at rest.

Learn to slow down and enjoy life. It's not only the scenery you miss by going too fast — you also miss the sense of where you are going and why.

(Eddie Cantor)

AT RISK: An exaggerated response to mental stress can cause blockages in blood vessels. A recent study reports that those who show the most extreme blood pressure responses on a mental-stress test had the thickest blockages in their carotid arteries. Stress response may turn out to be a new risk factor for heart disease and stroke.

(*Parade Magazine*, March 15, 1998)

PHYSICAL ISSUES NOT AN ISSUE

If you are inclined to blame your physical health for your lack of achievement or exercise in your life, you might first consider the story of David Connolly. Connolly was born with feet and leg deformities so severe that his legs had to be amputated just below his knees. But guess what? He walks, runs and dances with the help of prostheses. He's danced on Broadway, he sings professionally and, for the past three years has worked as an associate with the choreography of the Miss America pageant and other projects.

MUST NOT HAVE BEEN
HIS TIME TO GO

In Kenmore, NY, a 30-year old man leaped from a fourth story window and survived by landing on a car. He rode an elevator back up and repeated his suicide attempt, jumping from the same window and landing on the same car! Other than a broken wrist and ankle, he was in good shape. (*News & Observer*, Raleigh, NC, 4/6/92)

FOCUS ON THE HEALING

When Olympic Gold medal winner and professional ice skater Scott Hamilton was diagnosed with testicular cancer, he handled it with his typical pizzazz and gusto. After his initial shock and fear, he said to himself: "All right, this happened. What next? How do I fight it and beat it? Give me all the information and what it takes to get rid of this thing . . . I really wanted to consider this a very short and temporary part of my life. I never will focus on the negatives." (*The Associated Press*-9/18/97)

FROM "INTENSE" TO "AT EASE"

Tense your entire body, head to toe, squeezing all your muscles and hold it for about five seconds. Then very slowly begin to relax completely. Breathe easily. Tense yourself again and hold the tension for another five seconds before you relax again. Repeat the process once more. This technique forces you to feel the extreme opposites of bodily functioning - relaxation vs. tension.

IT'S ALL RELATED: Recent scientific evidence that lends support to a holistic view of the body is helping to move some mind-body therapies into the mainstream. Researchers have discovered that there is a continuous dialogue between the nervous, immune and endocrine systems, suggesting that emotions influence immunity - positive emotions may bolster it and negative emotions depress it.

The New York Times, Oct. 4, 1992

A TEST OF YOUR RECEPTIVENESS TO RELAXATION

Interlock your fingers in a prayer position, and hold them at nose level in front of your face, about 8 inches away. Extend your two index fingers and separate them. Staring at your fingers, repeat to yourself "Fingers, come together, fingers come together . . ." Continue thinking that phrase as you stare at your index fingers.

If your fingers mysteriously seem to come together with a will and power of their own, you are a prime candidate to benefit from meditation and relaxation exercises. If instead your index fingers became rigid and fixed, even shook a little, you have a strong degree of mental control, and may find meditation and relaxation activities to be stressful rather than calming.

JUST TWENTY MINUTES

Comptroller: I'm finding it really difficult to add exercise to my daily routine. Does twenty minutes of exercise three times a week really make that much of a difference?

Cher: It's the difference between a body that works for you and one that doesn't. It's *the* critical factor in long-term health.

Comptroller: Just twenty minutes three times a week? That's hard to believe.

Cher: You're not alone in your skepticism. There are lots of doubters who enjoy criticizing the benefits of tools such as walking, meditating, hiking, gardening, sitting quietly, practicing yoga, jogging, and the like. You don't doubt your ability to manage money, do you? Or liquefy assets? Or diversify your portfolio? Don't doubt the benefit of investing in your health. The ROI is just as real there.

KENNETH COOPER AND AEROBICS: In 1968, Dr. Kenneth Cooper thumbed through a dictionary, hunting for a word to describe his findings that vigorous exercise appeared to improve health dramatically. The word he found: aerobe — a microorganism that can live and grow only where free oxygen is present. He called his exercise program "aerobics."

In 1970, Dr. Cooper retired from the military to devote his career to the study of aerobic fitness. He does a radio interview almost every day, travels extensively, giving about 15 speeches a month and still sees patients. He has written 14 books, and owns his 30-acre, five building fitness compound in north Dallas.

His recommendations for physical activity: Walk two miles in less than 30 minutes, 3 times a week OR walk two miles in less than 45 minutes. The good doctor admits he's stumped by the question of how to motivate people to exercise before they become sick.

(Los Angeles Times, copied in N&O, Raleigh, NC
February 1, 1998)

SHALL WE DANCE?

Take a risk and sign up for dance lessons somewhere. It can be ballroom dancing, line dancing, tap, ballet or even shag. The purpose is to push yourself beyond your inhibitions and experience a whole new relationship with your body. Dance creates a body/soul communication, and teaches us how to focus on the moment. At the same time, dance lessons provide vigorous aerobic exercise.

My husband, Bil, and I began ballroom dancing, and discovered not only a great source of exercise, but also a wonderful avocation. We've competed as an amateur couple, performed choreographed routines for showcases, and brought fun into our relationship in amazing ways. We have surprised ourselves — not only with the dance moves we're able to perform — but with the joy and peace we are experiencing through our dance.

By the way, if you don't want to sign up for lessons, just pump up the music in the privacy of your own living room and make up your own routines. You'll discover a great release as well as a new companionship with your body!

Dance is one of the most powerful forms of magical ritual
… It is an outer expression of the inner spirit.
(Ted Andrews)

We ought to dance with rapture that we should be alive,
and in the flesh, and part of the living, incarnate cosmos.
(D. H. Lawrence)

Every day I count wasted in which there has been no
dancing.
(Friedrich Nietzsche)

NO PAIN, NO GAIN???

Construction Superintendent: I recently began working out in the gym, and keep hearing the phrase 'No Pain, No Gain'. How do you feel about that?

Cher: I think it is incredibly dangerous — and absolutely wrong! When your body expresses pain, it is crying out to you to pay attention! It's telling you that you are doing something incorrectly or inappropriate for you. Pain can be one of your most loyal and trustworthy allies, if only you will listen. When you experience pain, stop doing what you're doing. If you don't listen, your body will find other ways to scream its message.

Heel Appeal: According to the American Orthopedic Foot and Ankle Society, you can relieve heel pain by regularly stretching your Achilles tendon. Here's how: Stand about three feet from a wall and place your hands on the wall. Lean toward the wall — bringing one leg forward and bending your arms at the elbows. Keep your back and your back leg straight with your heel on the floor. If you're doing it right, you'll feel a gentle stretch in the calf muscle of your back leg. Hold the stretch for five seconds, then repeat with the other leg.

STATS TO PONDER AS YOU WANDER . . .

If you are resisting a regular, formal exercise program because you feel you don't need one, consider this. And while you're considering it, I recommend you walk around the block, up and down the stairs, or through the halls of your office.

A release from the American Heart Association reports that 20-30% of the U.S. population are so sedentary that they have a three- to four-times higher risk for developing heart disease than their more active counterparts. Physical inactivity has been upgraded from a 'contributing factor' for heart disease and stroke to a 'risk factor'.

A LITTLE SWEAT IS GOOD FOR YOU

Without hesitating one more minute, build moderate exercise into your weekly routine. Go ahead - do some jumping jacks (five to ten quick ones would be great) and touch your toes three or four times. Do it — before

you read any further. Put the book down and jump a little. I'll wait.

If you patronized me, you've just exercised today.
I'm not being condescending. Committing yourself to
routine exercise is one of the most important *life* decisions you'll ever make. There's a ton of research that
outlines the life-enriching effects of proper nutrition,
diet and exercise - so I won't preach, except to encourage you to adopt a lifestyle which improves your health
instead of disintegrates it.

Begin gently. Acquaint your doctor with your proposed exercise regimen. Get a nutritionist involved. Be
cautious of technological gimmickry. Consult with a
physical therapist and/or a professional fitness instructor.
Build or tone slowly. Learn how your body responds to
exercise. Look forward to a trimmer, firmer, healthier you.

STEP UP THE PACE

Do you find yourself feeling tired - worn out - too
exhausted to do anything? Here's a great technique to
help you feel more energized. Force yourself to get up
and walk somewhere - from your office to the restroom;
from the kitchen to the bedroom; around the block; up
and down the center of the mall. As you move, simply
walk 25% faster than you normally do.

You will discover that you can change your attitude
by changing your posture and the speed of your movement. So step up the pace, and enjoy the surge of energy
you'll experience!

By forcing ourselves to take action and 'do something'
when we feel too tired to move, we actually revitalize the
body, and open the floodgates for energy to flow into our
body.

DETERMINE YOUR METABOLIC RATE

This formula will help you determine the rate at which you burn calories. It gives you an estimated figure of how many calories you can eat without gaining weight. But remember — you have to be honest!

Step 1. *Determine Your Resting Metabolic Rate (RMR):*

MEN	WOMEN
Weight in pounds x 6.2 = X	Weight in pounds x 4.3 = X
Height in inches x 12.7 = Y	Height in inches x 4.3 = Y
Add X + Y + 65 = Z	Add X + Y + 655 = Z

(Yes, men is only 65 and women is 655.
This is *not* a typographical error!)

Age in years x 6.8 = Q	Age in years x 4.7 = Q
Z - Q = RMR	Z - Q = RMR

Step 2. *Determine Activity Level (AL)*

1.2 = Couch Potato
1.4 = Moderately Active
1.8 = Athlete Training Level

Step 3. *Determine Number of Calories You Can Eat Without Gaining Weight*

RMR x AL = # Calories You Burn on Average Day

FUEL UP IN THE MORNING

Too many people try to save calories by skipping breakfast — big mistake! Studies show that breakfast eaters tend to be leaner than non-breakfast eaters. They typically take in less fat and cholesterol all day! And, they tend to get more fiber.

Think for a moment about what you do when you are about to take a long trip in your car. One of the first things you do is fuel it up, so you know you're starting out with a full tank. You deserve to treat yourself as well as you do your car! But be smart about what you choose. Try whole grain cereals with skim milk; whole wheat toast with jelly; fresh fruit; a scrambled or poached egg; or a half a bagel with light cream cheese.

A RESTAURANT BATTLE PLAN

One of the toughest temptations to a good diet comes as we enter the portals of a restaurant. It is criminal how easy they make it to eat unhealthy — and how difficult it is to eat healthy. Recently Bil and I stayed in a hotel, where the restaurant did not have skim milk, light salad dressings or artificial sweetener. Unbelievable!

We've found we need to be on our guard when we travel, and have a battle plan ready to put in action as we enter a restaurant. Here are some of our most successful strategies:

- Order house salads with a light dressing. If no light dressing is available, use lemon juice. Always ask for the dressing on the side. Dip your fork into the dressing, then your salad. You enjoy the taste of the dressing without overdoing it.
- Select meat that is grilled, roasted, baked or broiled, and ask questions about how it is cooked. Ask to have it without the sauce or gravy, or with the sauce on the side.
- Choose vegetables that are steamed or broiled, without sauces or butter.
- Use a low-fat ranch-type dressing or salsa on your baked potato instead of butter.
- Avoid the bread basket! (This is my personal shortcoming! I love bread and will eat it all if they leave it there!)
- If you are eating in town, ask for a doggie bag when you order your food. As soon as the food is delivered, put half your meal in the doggie bag for

tomorrow's dinner. Most restaurants provide servings that are much too large. (Warning: Your waitperson will look at you like you are crazy when you do this!)

• Do not allow the waitperson to show you the dessert tray. Decide ahead of time if you are going to eat dessert. If so, cut your intake appropriately during the meal, and choose to split a dessert with others or select one that is somewhat healthy.

REMEMBER:
Nothing tastes as good as healthy feels!

When people consciously choose to neglect their bodies, they have decided to live in a waste dump.
(Bil Holton)

HEALTHY FOOD SUBSTITUTES

Try these substitutes as a way to cut the fat and calories without cutting the taste in your eating:

Instead of whole or 2% milk, use skim milk; instead of butter, use jelly; instead of potato chips, use pretzels; instead of alcohol, drink a glass of peach or pear juice spiked with some ginger ale.

BECOMING "CRAVING-WHYS"

Get wise about the whys of your cravings! According to several sources, there are psychological needs that create the physical food cravings you experience. The next time you get a craving, consider the possibility that the craving is telling you about some deeper need. In your Self-Development Journal, identify your food craving. Then review the following list and brainstorm ideas of issues in your life that could be creating the craving. Deal with that need, and the craving will ease.

CRAVING	MEANING
Sweets	Need for positive reinforcement; sweet words; good feedback
Crunchy	Need to release anger or aggression
Cheese/Dairy Products	Need for nurturing; time off to relax; be taken care of
Salty, Spicy Foods; Caffeine; Carbonated Beverages	Need for excitement; need to get out of ruts ("spice up your life!")
Breads; Pasta	Financial worries; concern about ability to support yourself (bread and dough: slang for money!)

> The American Medical Association reports that one study of 842 middle aged men found that those who ate the most fruits and vegetables substantially decreased their risk of stroke. Eating three additional servings per day decreased their risk by 22%.

SALT OF THE EARTH

About 75% of the sodium you eat comes from processed and fast food — not the salt shaker. The recommended daily maximum is 2,400 mg. The more preparation the food industry does for you, the higher the amount of sodium in the food. Consider: Canned tomato sauce contains 1,480 mg; turkey pot pie has 1,000 mg; canned chicken noodle soup a hefty 1,107 mg; and a dill pickle weighs in with 928 mg. 1 ounce of potato chips has 200 mg; while 1 ounce of twist pretzels has 505 mg.

Fast foods also contribute to your sodium intake. Specialty burgers with the special cheeses and sauce typically provide approximately 900-1800 mg of sodium, not to mention the fat involved! If you consumed a specialty burger, fries and a chocolate shake, you'd give your body a whopping 1400 mg of sodium in just one sitting! Stick with fresh and frozen foods as much as possible to avoid too much sodium in your diet.

TIPS TO REDUCE YOUR SODIUM INTAKE

- Make an Herb Shaker. Combine: 2 t. thyme; 1 1/2 t. sage; 2 t. rosemary; 2 1/2 t. marjoram; 2 1/2 t. savory. Use this to season vegetables, meats, fish or poultry.
- Always taste food before adding salt.
- Remove your salt shaker from the dinner table. You're less apt to use salt if you actually have to get up and get it.
- Make wiser choices in your snacks. Try fresh fruit and vegetables rather than munchies.
- Make your own casseroles rather than using the pre-packaged versions in the grocery store. If you really think about it, it doesn't take that much more energy or time to make a chicken, broccoli, rice casserole from scratch. The results not only provide less sodium and fat, they taste better, too!

TOO MUCH TV AND READING?

Research results from an Arizona State University study found women who spend the most time reading women's magazines and watching television are more likely than others to idealize thinness, dislike their bodies and show symptoms of eating disorders.

Put down that magazine — turn off that TV — and go for a long walk! Take a look at the real people in the real world, and get a realistic grip on your own self image. Look in the mirror — and if you don't like what you see there, realize that you *can* do something about it!

> Slogan for a Canadian funeral home chain:
> "Exercise. Eat well. Stay healthy. We can wait."

WATER, WATER EVERYWHERE

You hear it again and again — drink water. We know it, but most people fail to follow this excellent advice. In order to maintain hydration, you should drink eight 8-ounce glasses of water each day — more if you spend time outside. When children are active, they should get a water break every 20 minutes.

Don't wait until you feel thirsty to get a drink. By the time you feel thirsty, you've already lost 2 cups of water or more.

Drink water steadily throughout the day. Keep a bottle of water with you as you commute, at your desk, and through your activities. Sip on it all day.

Start and end the day with a serving of water to help make up for the loss of water while you sleep.

Cool water is absorbed more quickly than warm fluids and is better at keeping you hydrated than sports drinks. It may be better at cooling down an overheated body than any other beverage. (Scripps Howard News Service)

THE HOLTON TOE TO HEAD ROUTINE

If you spend a large portion of your day sitting behind a desk, you need a specific routine that forces you to get those muscles moving. Here's my routine, which you can perform several times a day standing right next to your desk. Do all the movements slowly and deliberately, enjoying the feel of those muscles stretching and celebrating movement.

Stand up straight and tall. Go up and down on your

toes ten times; then do ten partial knee bends, where you simply flex and unflex your knees slightly. Place the palms of your hands together and press hard for five seconds. Shake it out, then interlock your fingertips and pull them against each other for five seconds; shake out. Repeat five times.

Reach up and grab an imaginary rope above your head, and use all your muscles to act as if you are pulling yourself up that rope. You should feel the muscles in your sides stretch as you pull one hand over the other. Do this for ten seconds.

Now place your arms in front of you. Bend your elbows and pull back in rowing movement. Repeat for ten "rows." Then shrug and roll your shoulders several times. Slowly lower your head forward toward your chest, then gently roll your head toward your right shoulder. Hold this position, then gently roll your head forward toward your chest again. In a continuous movement, continue rolling your head gently toward your left shoulder, hold, then back to your chest. Repeat this neck roll three times. Do not rotate your head toward the back; it can cause pain and damage. Now shake your whole body a few times from head to toe (. . . and turn yourself around. That's what it's all about!)

You'll be amazed at how alert and energetic you feel after doing this simple series of stretches. I recommend doing it near a bookcase or file cabinet. That way, if someone walks by while you're reaching up to that "rope," you can just act like you're reaching for something off the top of the bookcase or cabinet!

Much of what passes for illness is a subconscious attempt to escape life's responsibilities.

(Catherine Ponder)

MELODIOUS HEALTH

Director of Corporate Communications: Cher, do you really think the healing properties of music are as effective as, say, aspirin or cough syrup?

Cher: Don't underestimate the power of music. It speaks to the wounds and the restlessness and the doubts and fears we have no words for. Religious leaders the world over have long known about the healing qualities of music. The act of singing and chanting our bodies back into atunement and harmony has always been practiced. Sound is primal. Melodious sound is therapeutic. Is it as effective as aspirin…or cough syrup, for curing ones ills? In some instances, I believe it is. Music soothes the emotions. The medical community is finally recognizing the impact emotions have on healing and recovery.

Surrounded by the right sounds, we can all be invigorated, energized and balanced.

(Dr. John Diamond)

A LIBRARY OF MUSIC MOOD MAKERS

Use music as a way to create the mood you desire. Build a library of tapes or CD's including three categories: Music to exercise by; music to make you feel happy (the kind you just have to sing along with); and music to soothe your soul.

A sampling from my library: Exercise music: John Tesh's The Games; Soundtrack from Rocky; Soundtrack from Fame. Positive attitude music: Celine Dion; Jim Croce; Soundtracks from variety of Broadway musicals. Soothe the soul music: Soundtrack from Out of Africa; Pachabel's Cannon; Emile Pandolfi; Steve Hall.

Music is very personal, so it's important to make your own selections. Have them categorized and organized so you can reach for what you need, and find it instantly. You'll be amazed at how music can move you to action or calm you.

BODY WISDOM

When it comes to overall health, moderation is the best policy in eating, drinking, exercising and sleeping. Taking care of the physical you is one of the best investments you'll ever make. Physical fitness is paramount to sustained health and sustained health is necessary for quality of life.

All of us shed skin, lose hair, transform brain cells, redistribute weight, digest food and live in our body — the only body we have. Although sometimes parts of our body might be replaced, most of our body will remain intact, for better or for worse. So it just makes good sense to take care of our bodies.

Respect yourself enough to take care of yourself. Pay attention to your body's wisdom. Listen to its advice. Beware of its messages. If it says: *"That hurts,"* — stop hurting yourself. If it admits: *"I'm tired,"* — slow down, rest, relax. If it asks: *"What are you doing to me?"* — assess your habits, examine your motives.

TAKE A SOBERING FIELD TRIP

If you become a little depressed about how life is treating you, visit any one of these six places: an orphanage, the burn ward or cancer ward at a hospital, a children's hospital, a veteran's hospital, a retirement home, or a hospice. You'll probably see people, young and old, worse off than you. If that doesn't help you put things in perspective, visit a funeral home.

You may want to have someone visit these places

with you. You'll both be deepened by the experience…
and appreciate your own situations a little better. Life …
and health … and mobility … and well-being are precious
things. Each of us has our own challenges. Be thankful
your fretfulness and slight depression are all you have to
deal with today. Say a prayer for those people you've
just observed, and then leap with joy at only having to
handle your own circumstances. Decide to look at life
more positively. Move about with more grace and thank-
fulness.

COULD YOU BE THE MATTER WITH YOU?

Sales Director: Cher, I read somewhere that illness and
disease — even accidents — are inside jobs. That we
cause them ourselves. Do you think that's true?

Cher: I don't think we cause *all* our sickness and diseases
by any means, but I do believe we bring many illnesses on ourselves. For example, arthritis has been linked
to feeling unloved or overly-criticized. It has also been
associated with rigidity and resentment toward being
forced to change. A broken heart in romantic pursuits
or extreme personal disappointments can lead to heart
failure. Some cancers are linked to deep hurts…or
long-standing resentments. Carrying hatreds or allowing grief to eat away at you are also associated with
cancer. Strokes occur when people give up on themselves or resist unwanted change with every fiber of
their being. Stroke patients seem to reject life. Many
studies have linked the strong feeling of not being
good enough or repressed inadequacy as the cause of
ulcers. Being overly anxious to please everyone is also
linked to ulcers and stomach problems.

Sales Director: What about pain? You know, pain in
general?

Cher: Pain with no perceivable cause, no visible injuries or physical trauma generally means guilt is involved…and guilt always seeks punishment. Back pain, for example, is linked to over-concern for money or feeling pressured by lack of money or over-all support.

Sales Director: Do you think if people knew this, they'd take better care of themselves?

Cher: I think if people knew themselves, they'd take better care of everything.

PUT NEGATIVITY IN REMISSION

Deepak Chopra, a renowned New England endocrinologist who is researching the mind-body connection reports that a major study of 400 spontaneous remissions of cancer found that all the patients had only one thing in common — every person had changed attitude before the remission occurred, finding some way to become hopeful, courageous and positive.

SOME FINAL THOUGHTS ABOUT PHYSICAL HEALTH

Your body is the ground metaphor of your life, the expression of your existence. It is your Bible, your encyclopedia, your life story.

(Gabrielle Roth)

We create every so-called "illness" in our body.

(Louise Hay)

Repeating positive affirmations to yourself, visualizing health, wealth and happiness; praying petitions of thanksgiving and protection are all instances of doing within while you're doing without.

(Bil Holton)

Graveyards are full of indispensable [people].

(Charles DeGaulle)

Human intention has been shown to interact with matter at a distance, affecting the particles in a cloud chamber, crystals and the rate of radioactive decay...An intention to heal has been demonstrated to alter enzymes, hemoglobin values, and the hydrogen-oxygen bond in water.

(Marilyn Ferguson)

The only reason I would take up jogging is so...I would hear heavy breathing again.

(Erma Bombeck)

And that's the way it is.

(Walter Cronkite)

§ § § § § § § § §

And now . . .
. . . on to our mental health.

The AC/DC Continuum

Imagine a Continuum with AC at one end and DC at the other end (See Diagram). Everything we experience in life falls somewhere on this continuum. The AC represents things over which we have little or no control. For example, we are stuck in traffic, the computer is down, we must care for elderly parents, we receive negative information related to a health condition, we don't like the style of our new manager, or we aren't selected for a proposal we submitted. The possibilities are limitless. The key is to ask ourselves "Can we change it?" If the answer is NO, then we must use the AC side: Accept and Cope. This means we assess ways to manage ourselves within the situation, to maintain our sanity and keep our perspective.

The DC side represents those things over which we **do** have control: our habits; our thoughts; skill development; giving feedback to others; taking risks; how we respond to situations. If we don't like the situation we must Dare to Change . . . take the necessary steps to create a change toward what we want. The secret is to understand where an issue falls on the continuum, so we don't waste a lot of time and energy fighting something over which we have no control.

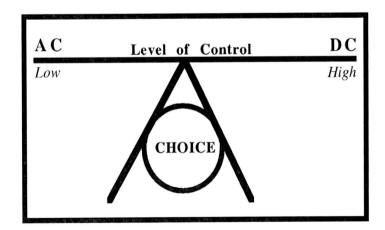

Let's take a simple example: getting stuck in traffic. I don't know about you, but this is one thing that really irritates me. First, let's evaluate where it falls on our AC/DC Continuum. Since I'm stuck there, the traffic isn't moving, and there's nothing I can do about it, it would fall on the AC side: an area where I have little or no control over the situation.

Next I need to Accept the situation. This means I actually have to talk to myself: "O.K., Cher, you are stuck in this traffic jam. No one's moving. You can't go anywhere or do anything about it. Accept it and let it go."

Now I need to look for ways to cope with the situation in a positive way. For example, I can play music I enjoy; plan my calendar for the day; make calls on my cell phone; read (at least while the traffic is at a standstill! Once it starts up again, I recommend putting the reading material away!); meditate; etc. If I do any one of these things, what is my level of control? Very High! So essentially what I have done is taken a situation where I have very little or no control, and made a choice to do something over which I have very high control. This perception of high control makes me feel much better. While it doesn't *change* the situation, it has a dramatic impact on how I *handle* the situation.

The power comes from the CHOICES we make — and there are *always* choices! I have found that when I am most frazzled and frustrated, if I check it against this continuum, sure enough, I'm trying to change something that belongs on the AC side.

Apply this Harmony Principle :
Dare to Change or Accept and Cope!
The power is in your choice!

You are everything you choose to be. You are as unlimited as the endless universe.
                                        (Shad Helmstetter)

CHOOSE TO HAVE A PITY PARTY . . . BUT TIME IT

My Program Administrator, Nancy Eubanks, shared this story with me. When she was in the hospital, recovering from some very serious surgery, she found herself feeling quite depressed. A nurse entered her room and caught her crying.

"What's wrong?" she asked.

"Well, I guess I'm just feeling sorry for myself," Nancy replied tearfully.

The nurse surprised her with her comeback. Her eyes twinkled as she looked Nancy right in the eyes and said, "Well, Nancy, it's OK to have pity parties here. In fact, we encourage it! People need to get those negative feelings out. But we do require that you put a time limit on your pity party. So, how much time do you think you'll need for this pity party?"

This really threw Nancy for a loop, and she said, somewhat hesitatingly, "I don't know. Maybe a half an hour?"

The nurse smiled and said, "Fine. You go ahead and have a real good pity party, but in a half hour I want to see you out in the hall, and we'll take a walk."

With that, the nurse left the room. Nancy shared that she began to feel depressed again, and even cried a little bit, but she also noticed that she kept looking at her watch! And sure enough, in 30 minutes, she met the nurse for a walk around the nurse's station.

Go ahead and allow yourself the luxury of a little negativity — but put a time limit on your pity party!

The mind and body are like parallel universes. Anything that happens in the mental universe must leave tracks in the physical one.

(Deepak Chopra, MD)

A DOUBLE DOZEN

The purpose of this activity is to spawn life enriching insights. You'll need a notebook (or a laptop or desk computer), pen or pencil, and courage. Select one of the multiple listings below and generate a double dozen (In case you're not a math wizard, that would be 24!) items for that listing. Select a different one each month. Be sure to complete each list. Keep the list in front of you the entire month. As you focus on it, ask yourself what messages you are receiving from your higher self. What do your entries tell you about yourself, your interests, your needs, your desires? What changes could you make in your lifestyle to accommodate some of the a-ha's you've experienced? What are you learning about you?

Every month, choose a new Double Dozen topic. Keep all your lists, and at the end of the year, review your entries and celebrate your growth.

This sounds like a simple exercise, but I promise, it's provocative, highly introspective and soul-enriching.

I have included more than twelve entries so you may choose those which especially interest you during the next twelve months. Or, feel free to come up with your own!

- A Double Dozen things I do well.
- A Double Dozen things I'd like to know more about.
- A Double Dozen accomplishments I'm proud of.
- A Double Dozen things I'm thankful for.
- A Double Dozen things that once frightened me, but don't anymore.
- A Double Dozen things I value in life.
- A Double Dozen famous people I'd like to meet.
- A Double Dozen principles to live by.
- A Double Dozen responsibilities I wouldn't want to have.
- A Double Dozen things that make me laugh or smile.

- A Double Dozen places I'd like to visit or live for a while.
- A Double Dozen adjectives I could use to describe myself.
- A Double Dozen inventions that have made my life easier.
- A Double Dozen quotes that have changed my life.
- A Double Dozen wishes I'd like to make.
- A Double Dozen things I've done before (but haven't done in a while) that I'd like to do again.
- A Double Dozen things I could learn from children.
- A Double Dozen lessons that were tough, but I'm glad I learned.
- A Double Dozen things I enjoy doing (even if I don't take time to do them anymore).

"SLO-MO"

We live in a world of speed: we have microwave food, Jiffy Popcorn; 30-minute pizza; instant credit; quick lanes at the grocery store; and fast food restaurants. It's instant gratification…and life whirls by in a blur, leaving us feeling dazed and confused. This technique is designed to help you re-claim a feeling of control over life. There are three variations:

1. *Deliberately choose to move at a slower pace.* Choose a longer line at the grocery store, or stay behind a car moving slower than you prefer. As you do this, say to yourself: "I choose to slow down, relax and enjoy this moment."

2. **Really** *look at something.* Do you realize how often we move through life, ignoring the beauty of scenery, a gorgeous sunset, or a friendly face? Do what poet William Carlos Williams calls "caressing the details." Slow down and move your eyes slowly over the scene around you. Allow yourself to truly experience

each object, each element of the scenery, the idio-syncrasies of people around you.

3. *Move in slow motion.* (Note: I'd definitely recom-mend trying this one in the privacy of your home, when no one else is there.) As you perform your regular tasks, simply move more slowly, making every movement deliberate and exact. You'll be amazed how intricate simple tasks really are! Don't be surprised if you have difficulty doing easy things, like tying your shoes, or writing a check. We do so much unconsciously. This simple tech-nique will increase your appreciation for what you do, while it calms and relaxes you.

THE APOSTROPHE EFFECT

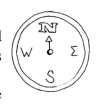

We all know how important it is to set goals…and write them down. But let's face it. Everyone experiences times when the goals they have set seem impossible … out of reach … beyond their capabilities. The Apostrophe Effect can help inspire you to look beyond the outward appearances of barriers and frustrations, opening your mind to creative ways to achieve your goals.

On a blank sheet of paper, write out your goal clear-ly and specifically. Underneath it, in big, bold letters, print the word IMPOSSIBLE. This is the Reality Factor. You are putting what you are thinking into writing so it's out of your head and down on paper. Rather than men-tally fighting it, you're acknowledging it.

Now, take a moment to look at what you've written. Own it. Accept it. Then, take a colored pen and make a big apostrophe between the I and the M in the word "Impossible." What does it say now? **I'M POSSIBLE.** This simple change creates a dramatic shift in your thinking. All of a sudden that goal is looking at you say-ing, "I'm possible. Stretch your thinking. Consider options. There is a way to make this happen!"

So, when you get sidelined by a belief that your dream is impossible, apply the Apostrophe Effect and get back on track.

 What we need is more people who specialize in the impossible.

(Theodore Roethke)

SHINING MOMENTS

As you think back over your life, list a hundred of your favorite wins and when they happened. You know, the things you did well, the ones you're most proud of, your *shining moments*. They can range from putting a piece of candy back instead of stealing it, to writing a novel, finishing a major project, losing weight, telling the truth, facing a fear, running a marathon or starting your own business.

Realistically, you probably won't be able to think of 100 in one sitting. (If you can, congratulations! *You* need to write a book!) Keep this Shining Moments List where you can see it and add items as they pop into your head (and believe me, they'll come at the strangest times!)

The purpose of this activity is to help you appreciate you. We focus so much on what we've done wrong. We weigh ourselves down with regrets, disappointments, and might-have-beens. This activity will help balance the scale, and let you celebrate the positive, thoughtful, wise-choice part of you that often gets neglected.

LET SOMEONE IN FRONT OF YOU IN LINE

Whether you're in a grocery store line, in traffic, the movie ticket line or any other place where waiting your turn is a frustrating fact of life, let someone in front of you. This small act can give you a tremendous feeling of time control, and is a great attitude builder — for yourself and the other person!

EXERCISE THE POWER OF CHOICE

Quality Engineer: Are you suggesting that the power of choice is one of the keys to success, anyone's success?

Cher: Exactly. I wish people really believed that, because wherever you are is the entry point into your next experience.

Quality Engineer: How can I become aware of using my power of choice?

Cher: Try this awareness process. Every time you find yourself feeling frustrated about doing something, ask yourself: "Is this a choice?" If the answer is yes (and it usually is!), then affirm: "The choice is mine!" Then say, "I choose . . ." and put your choice into words, followed by "because . . .," which justifies in your mind the decision you just made.

5-10-15 TECHNIQUE FOR DEPRESSION

Even the most positive people occasionally need an attitude adjustment! We all experience times when life becomes a little overwhelming, and things don't go the way we expected. We get irritated, negative, and even depressed. The 5-10-15 Technique provides a strategy to acknowledge the negative emotions, then take control over them. The entire technique takes 30 minutes, but it's time well spent when you discover you're in a really bad mood. Warning: You will not feel like using this technique when you most need it! But force yourself! You'll be glad you did.

Step 1:   Set a timer for 5 minutes. Use this 5 minutes to be as negative and depressed as you want. Give in to the feelings and emotions. Scream . . . gripe . . . complain . . . whine . . . cry . . . whatever you feel like doing. This is your time for guilt-free negativity.

Step 2:   When the timer goes off, reset it for 10 minutes. This is your 10-minute transition period. You're still allowed to be negative, but now you must counter your depression and whining with some rational positive thinking. Begin the process of talking to yourself about your negativity, and telling yourself to change your attitude. Don't be hard on yourself, just be calm and rational. Say things like "It's OK to be depressed for a while, but now it's time to take control. Think about your blessings. Focus on the good stuff. Don't let this depression get you down."

Step 3:   When the timer goes off, reset it for 15 minutes. This is your Rebound period. During the next 15 minutes, give yourself up to positive thoughts and words. Repeat positive affirmations. Sing. Identify all your positive traits. Count your blessings. If you find yourself slipping back into a negative cloud, catch yourself. Acknowledge the slip, and reward yourself for noticing it and returning to positive thoughts.

By the time the timer goes off this time, you will be amazed at the change you have created in your own attitude. It really is that easy (and that tough!)

PLEASANT REMINDERS

Step back into one of your pleasant moments from the past and relive it fondly. Experience the delightful event again. Remember how you felt, who you were with, where you were, why you were there. Reconnect with everything about that special moment. Replay the sights and sounds, the moods, the good time you had.

If you're still in the mood, pull up another nostalgic reminder. Bask in the fond memory. Enjoy yourself enjoying yourself.

Remembered joys enrich the present. They take our minds off our present labors and ground us to that part of us that knows what joy feels like. Pleasant memories fortify us from today's labors. They center us. They remind us we are capable of feeling joy and experiencing inner peace.

A bend in the road is not the end of the road . . . unless you fail to make the turn.

(Successories Plaque)

WHAT CAUSES YOUR STRESS?

Remember: YOU are the main source of stress in your life. It is your perception of events and people around you that creates an internal response. You cannot always control the situation you are in, or the people with whom you must interact, but you CAN control your response. The principle: Put your stress on wellness!

ATTITUDE OF GRATITUDE

At the end of each day, record in a notebook those things for which you are grateful. It can range from big stuff (like getting a promotion) to small things easily over-

looked (a compliment from an unexpected source or discovering a quarter on the ground). Try to get at least one
entry per day. On those "bad" days, it's reassuring to go
back through your entries and remind yourself of all
you've had to be grateful for.

The Attitude of Gratitude List works for specific
events, too. When you find yourself in the midst of a
frustrating, irritating or negative situation, simply pause
for a moment and ask yourself: What about this can I
find to be grateful for?

DELAYED FLIGHT

One of my "Marker Events" that really sold me on
the power of the Gratitude List happened in December
of 1986. I was flying from Cincinnati back home to
Raleigh, NC. It was a late evening flight, to get me home
for a luncheon speech I was scheduled to give the next
day.

There was a plane change in Baltimore. That's
where it happened! We sat on the runway for nearly two
hours before they finally determined that the plane was-
n't going anywhere that night. It was 11:15 p.m., I was
exhausted and concerned about flight arrangements for
the next day. I finally got through the long line, and
found myself in a nearby Comfort Inn for the night. I
still have the Attitude of Gratitude List I made that night,
on a piece of hotel stationery. Some of the things about
the incident for which I could be grateful: the problem
with the plane occurred on the ground rather than in the
air; the airline put us up in a hotel as opposed to making
us sleep on the floor in the airport; the hotel had hot
water for a nice shower; I was able to get my husband on
the phone before he had left for the airport to pick me
up; I didn't have checked luggage, so I had control of
my suitcase; I got to hear Gary Morris sing a fabulous

rendition of O Holy Night on the Tonight show; and I got a great story for my speeches!

Just reviewing that list made me feel better about the whole situation, and I got a great night's sleep. Additionally, I got a flight that allowed me to get back to Raleigh in time to make my next day's commitment!

SOME FACTS ABOUT FEAR

- Fear makes pain hurt more. University students in various experiments were examined with an algesimeter, which measures pain thresholds. The research showed that when they felt fear, their pain threshold lowered significantly, making them more sensitive to pain and injury.
- Brave people are not without fear. If a person knows no fear, he or she is foolhardy, not brave. Feelings of fear often serve as warnings of danger. Courage is the ability to move ahead in spite of the fear one is feeling.
- Ignoring the source of your fear will not make it go away. All the research studies indicate that gradual exposure to the things you fear will help you overcome the phobias. Ignoring it only increases its hold on you.
- Laughing at your fears is a great way to conquer them. Psychiatric studies show that learning to laugh at your fears decreases their power to frighten you. Humor is an excellent way to share your fears with others, and laugh together.
- The more you enjoy life, the less you fear death. Studies at Vanderbilt University show that people whose lives lack meaning and purpose have the greatest fear of death.

(Reported by John Eppingham)

MEMORY LANE

Divide a piece of paper into five parts by drawing vertical lines from top to bottom. Label the paper as matrixed below and answer each of the life review questions.

Life Review Questions	Ages	1-10	11-15	16-21	22-30	30-39
Where did you live?						
Favorite family members?						
Favorite friends?						
Favorite foods/drinks?						
Favorite music/books/ movies?						
Favorite toys/games?						
Favorite clothing?						
Favorite hobbies/ interests/dream job?						

Using additional sheets of paper, move through your life in ten-year increments up to your current age. Answer the same questions. Enjoy your trip down memory lane. What have you learned about yourself from this self portrait? How can you use it to enrich your life? What themes do you see emerge? In what respects have you changed or stayed the same? What would you like to recapture? What would you like to forget? What life lessons came with the bad experiences? The good experiences? How have you grown?

Life can only be understood backward, but it must be lived
forward.

(Niels Bohr)

PARENTAL INFLUENCE

Complete the following statement. Take time right now to do it. If you decide not to do it now, schedule time for it later. It's worth your time and introspection.

One of the most important things my parents ever told me or did for me was

———————————————————

———————————————————

———————————————————

———————————————————

Step two may be a little tougher. If one or both of your parents is still alive, call them right now and share with them what you wrote. Then thank them for their positive influence in this area.

COLOR ANALYSIS

What is your favorite color? What do you have that is that color? When did you first realize it was your favorite color? How do you feel around that color? Describe yourself in or around that color. What do you think that color means in relation to your evolving personality?

LESSON FROM GONE WITH THE WIND

During the filming of *Gone With the Wind*, the "Burning of Atlanta" scene was the first to be shot — without actors. Old sets were burned to make room for the set to be designed for the other scenes of the movie.

The message: Out of the ashes of past situations and experiences can come the new beginnings for great scenes in your life. Be willing to burn those "old sets" from your past that no longer serve a purpose, and make room for new and wonderful things in your experience.

JUST SAY NO

Saying no to someone or something can be the ultimate choice in self-care. Don't be afraid to say no when the situation justifies it. Otherwise, you are saying yes to stress and inner frustration.

LETTING GO

Data Processing Manager: Cher, I know you're here on some other training program today, but I just had to tell you. I took a pick-up truck-load of stuff to Goodwill last week as a result of your seminar. I feel so much lighter and more energetic. Thank you for helping me unclutter my life.

Cher: That's great! There's something about recirculating the old and unused that liberates us, isn't there? One of the clearest signals that something psychologically healthy is afoot is the impulse to reposition furniture, sort through and discard old clothing and belongings, and purge garages and attics.

Data Processing Manager: That's where I'm starting next — the garage. I've got a two-car garage that has everything in it but the cars.

Cher: Hooray! As you ease out of your old self, honor your past interests, hobbies and relationships. Recirculate them with the dignity they deserve. It's freeing, isn't it?"

Data Processing Manager: Amazingly so! I was a little skeptical at first, but I told my wife about your seminar…and she's the one who decided we should try it. I'm glad we did.

Cher: Maybe we should call it spring forward cleaning. Have fun reclaiming your garage.

You have to believe in yourself, that's the secret — feel the exuberance that comes from utter confidence in yourself. Without it, you go down in defeat.

(Charlie Chaplin)

RECYCLE THINGS YOU AREN'T USING

Go through a drawer, a closet or one of those boxes in your garage or attic. Get rid of anything you haven't used in two years. Give it to someone who can use it, donate it to your favorite charity, or throw it away. By creating some space, you will feel more in harmony with your surroundings.

POSITIVE WORDS CREATE
POSITIVE ATTITUDES

One of the principles of good mental health is the fact that our feelings follow our words. If you don't believe me, try this: Make a list of negative words (ugly; failure; exhausted; angry; terrified) and a list of positive words (beautiful; success; energetic; thrilled; excited). Say each list out loud, with feeling, and become aware of how your body reacts as you read. Make it a habit to focus on saying strong positive words, especially when you least feel like doing it!

NEGATIVITY IS OVER-DONE

Medical Researcher: Isn't positive thinking over-cooked? How long has it been preached by Peale? Fifty years?

Cher: Dr. Norman Vincent Peale is certainly the one you think of when someone mentions positive thinking. I had the opportunity of hearing Dr. Peale speak, and he said the reason he kept preaching positive thinking is because, believe it or not, there were still some negative thinkers out there!

Medical Researcher: So how can we be positive thinkers without being seen as unrealistic or impractical?

Cher: Positive thinking does *not* mean Rose-Colored Glasses. It means focusing on what you *can* do rather than what you can't do. It means reviewing your options instead of counting the roadblocks. It means looking ahead with hope rather than looking back with regret and despair. Positive thinking is really a state of mind that permeates your life, and keeps you actively moving ahead. As for Dr. Peale's message being over-cooked, I believe the opposite is true. Negativity is over-done.

Medical Researcher: I agree. But as you know, Cher, most of my work involves the rigors of the scientific method. My job is to replicate findings. I've got to remain objective. I've got to look for experimental error...What was missed ... mistakes ... bias. So sometimes I *have* to focus on the negative.

Cher: I understand. Unfortunately, we have been socialized to believe that negativity means being realistic and looking at things in a positive light means we're unrealistic. I'm referring to the laboratory we call life where the variables are endless and the controls non-existent. Dr. Peale's message is just as important today as it was fifty years ago…and will be fifty years from now.

An optimist laughs to forget; a pessimist forgets to laugh.
(Tom Nansbury)

GLAMOUR GRAMMAR

Sell yourself on yourself! Emphasize your good qualities by speaking highly of yourself, especially when you're feeling down. Heighten your own morale by talking positively about yourself. Here's how.

Run through the alphabet and identify positive words beginning with each letter. Then preface each word with the phrase *I am.* For example: *I am* attractive. *I am* brilliant. *I am* creative. *I am* daring. *I am* enthusiastic. Be a legend in your own mind.

By the way, this is a great technique when you're stuck in traffic. Check out the license plate on the car in front of you. For each letter on the plate, come up with as many positive words (remember to keep them positive!) as you can. Say them out loud. You'll feel your frustration begin to evaporate.

Repeat these positive phrases to yourself as often as you can throughout the day. Use them as affirmations. If you recite them often enough and long enough, you'll start to notice a difference in the way you see yourself. You'll see a definite shift in your attitudes, capabilities and actions.

To speak of 'mere words' is much like speaking of 'mere dynamite'.
(C.J. Ducasse)

GET UN-RUT-BOUND

If you're a house plant lover, then you're familiar with the concept of being root-bound. This occurs when a plant has outgrown its pot. The roots are still trying to grow, but having nowhere to go, begin to wrap around the plant, eventually strangling itself. To solve the problem, all you have to do is re-pot the plant, giving the roots more room to grow.

We are just like plants — except that we get rut-bound. We allow ourselves to stagnate in the same routine, with no opportunity to have fresh new experiences. For example, I have friends who always go to the same restaurant, sit at the same table, and order the same food from the menu. Talk about ruts! Start now to break the routines, get un-rut-bound so you can stretch and grow as a person!

> *If they made a movie of your life,*
> *what would the title be?*

52 VACATIONS A YEAR

How do 52 vacations a year sound? Not a bad benefit, right? Why not give it to yourself, as a way to become un-rut-bound? Here's the challenge: Force yourself, once a week, to do something different from your usual routine. Some of my favorite 'Rut-Bound Busters' are: Walk around the house barefooted; enjoy an afternoon snooze in the hammock; play a game with the intent to lose instead of win; brush your teeth with your non-dominate hand; if you like meat, go vegetarian for a day; print or sign your name using your other hand; change your hair style; drive home a different way from work or the grocery store; get dressed putting your other hand through the sleeve first; call someone you've had a long-standing grudge with and reconcile your differences; eat at a new restaurant; visit a local tourist site you've never seen.

I won't belabor the point — you get the idea. Do something different, vary routines, eliminate old habits, revive yourself. And if you really feel adventuresome, try an Indiana Jones Experience (outlined later in this chapter).

WHAT HAVE YOU TASTED OF LIFE?

Life is filled with wonderful opportunities and experiences. Most people have done a lot more than they realize that is interesting, different and fun. We just tend to take it for granted, and look longingly at other people, wishing we could be like them.

Take a few minutes to evaluate your own experiences of "tasting" life. Make a list of everything you have done, places you've visited, foods you've tasted, sports you've experienced, instruments you've played, people you've met, etc. Reach into the recesses of your memory, and see how long a list you can come up with. You will probably amaze yourself! Share your list with other people, and see how they begin to admire you for some of the things you've done!

Life is like an international smorgasbord, and most people keep eating the fried chicken!

THE POWER OF ONE PERSON'S "VACATION"

I received a letter from a participant in one of my workshops who shared a powerful story. While I can't verify it, there seems no reason that he would have lied since I don't know him and he'll probably never see me again.

He admitted to being a rather structured soul, who liked routines in his life. After hearing my speech, he decided to try the 52 vacations. Because he was not adaptable to major change, he decided to start with something simple — driving a different way home from work. On this new, spontaneous route, he noticed a house with a For Sale sign in front of it. I could feel his excitement through the pages of his letter as he shared that he and his wife had been looking for a new home for several months, but had not been able to find what they were looking for. They'd sketched a picture of what they wanted and had it posted on their refrigerator, along with a list of the features they felt were important. So far, no luck.

Now comes the goose-bump part. The house he saw on his spontaneous drive home from work was exactly what they were looking for — down to a swing set in the backyard! He ended his letter by saying: "I am pleased to tell you that we are now living in that house — our dream home!"

THE RUT OF UNCHALLENGED RULES

I heard a woman being interviewed on a television show. She was describing a frightening event that she'd experienced. She had stopped at a traffic light; a car pulled up behind her and two men got out. They ran up on either side of her car and demanded that she open the window. They went so far as to actually rock her car back and forth. As she described her terror, the interviewer asked what I thought to be a very interesting question. "Why didn't you just hit the gas and get out of there?" Her reply? "Oh, I couldn't. The light was still red." Question the rules that run your life!

CHILDHOOD SNAPSHOTS

We can learn a lot from our childhood. People often say they don't really remember much about their childhood, but usually it's because they just haven't tried. Sometimes it's because the memories are painful. There may be unhealed wounds that need to be addressed, or inaccurate memories that need to be painted with a coat of reality. There may be lessons that can speed our journey to inner peace and well being. Spend time alone filling in the blanks. Skip any that do not apply, or don't seem to conjure up any memories. Enjoy the trip back into your childhood. If you want company, ask a trusted friend to accompany you.

Years 1 - 5

What I remember about my favorite playmate is _____

_____

My house was _____

_____

My favorite toy was my favorite because _____

_____

I remember liking to visit _____

_____

My brother was _____

_____

My sister used to always _____

_____

I was happiest when my parents _____

_____

My favorite bedtime story was _____

_____

One of the fondest memories of my pet was _____

_____

All serious daring starts from within.

(Eudora Welty)

SING A LITTLE SONG . . .

Just open your mouth and sing whatever song comes to mind! Grab a hairbrush, pretend it's a microphone and put your whole body into your performance. Do this in front of a mirror, and you may be tempted to sign up for Star Search!

MAKE UP A SONG

This strategy is one of those that sounds weird, but trust me! It is amazing! When you find yourself feeling depressed or frustrated, think of a well-known simple song. Examples are Row, Row, Row Your Boat; Take Me Out To The Ball Game; or Three Blind Mice. Using that well-known tune, create your own song, describing your feelings or problems. Then sing it with gusto!

An example (to the tune of Row, Row, Row Your Boat):

> I feel so mad inside I really want to scream!
> How can I handle this stupid deadline
> This goal is just a dream!

To take the technique a quantum leap forward, develop another verse to express a solution to the problem. Continuing with my example:

> I have to work real late to get this project done.
> I'll concentrate and I promise myself
> When I'm done I'll have some fun!

Use music to lift your spirits. Sufi master Hazret Inayat Khan said that there is nothing better than music as a means for the upliftment of the soul. Shakespeare wrote: The man that hath no music in himself/Nor is not moved with concord of sweet sounds/Let no such man be trusted. I love to quote the Bible verse in Psalms 100 that says "Make a joyful noise unto the Lord!" Notice it doesn't say the noise has to be in tune!

Music speaks to the wounds we have no words for.
(Julia Cameron)

STRENGTH OF CHARACTER

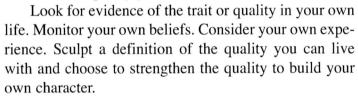

Dedicate the next twelve months to a close examination of your own character, your core values, your beliefs. Be willing to examine the real you. Examine each of the 12 concepts listed below for a month. Develop a concise definition. Study it. Live with it. Read quotations and illustrations on the subject by famous people. As thoroughly as possible, sift through the literature. Interview people who have faced challenges and exhibited the quality you are focused on.

Look for evidence of the trait or quality in your own life. Monitor your own beliefs. Consider your own experience. Sculpt a definition of the quality you can live with and choose to strengthen the quality to build your own character.

Start a notebook or computer file. One section or folder for each quality. Record your insights. Do some soul searching. Probe. Chisel away at your facade. Decide to be a better edition of yourself.

Choice	Fear
Success	Failure
Destiny	Talent
Wealth	Pain
Sacrifice	Freedom
Family	Health

True life is lived when tiny changes occur.
(Leo Tolstoy)

COPING WITH REALITY

In Garden City, Kansas, Sergeant Kirk Hutchinson had an excellent opportunity to practice the art of flexibility in coping with reality. He received a call on Monday, December 11, 1995 that his Division would be activated, and he was scheduled to leave for Bosnia on Saturday, December 16. Rather than cursing his misfortune at missing Christmas, he and his wife, along with their five children, celebrated their Christmas on Friday, December 15, opening gifts and creating a wonderful memory for them all. For them it was the experience of the holiday, not a specific day that was important!

HEAD SHOT

Have a studio-quality photo made. Ask the professional photographer to take several poses. Make sure the talent (that's you) looks your best. Ladies, sport your new do. Gentlemen, show 'em your best side - and smile.

Have the photographer take both color and black and white shots. Frame the full colored ones, run twenty or so of the 4 X 6 black and whites. Use them on your specially-printed personal letterheads, note paper or note cards. Your stock of black and whites will also come in handy as promo shots for community and club announcements in the local paper or for trade association and convention bulletins that feature you as one of the officers or speakers.

Place the framed photos where family and friends can see them. Use them to remind yourself how nice you can look when you want to. Imitate the beautiful you and the good-looking you in the photo. Endorse your good looks.

Why not be oneself? That is the whole secret of a successful appearance. If one is a greyhound, why try to look like a Pekingese?

(Edith Sitwell)

HUMAN WORTH

Do you know who you are? Have you any idea how important you are? How well do you know yourself? Your strengths? Your weaknesses? Your capabilities? Your worth? I agree with Swiss psychologist, Carl Jung, who said:

People will do anything, no matter how absurd, in order to avoid facing their own souls. They will practice … yoga …, observe a strict regimen of diet, learn theosophy by heart, or mechanically repeat mystic texts … all because they cannot get on with themselves and have not the slightest faith that anything useful could ever come out of their own souls.

And I agree with a similar, more economical statement by Mahatma Gandhi: *You must move beyond the illusion of your own insignificance.*

BE A "CAN-GURU"

There are so many people who are ready to tell us why we can't do something. One of the most popular phrases in any discussion about goals and dreams is: "You can't do that because . . ."

Become known as a "Can-Guru" — a person wise enough to focus on how things CAN be done. Make your mascot a kangaroo, always jumping in to claim how something can be accomplished — willing to support another person's dream.

Don't forget to be a "Can-Guru" in your own life, too. When your inner critic begins to tell you that you can't do something, fight back with the words, "Oh, yes I can!" Then hop to it, and take action to make it happen.

It is dangerous to value what you don't do, and to do what you don't value.

(Matt Weinstein)

LITERARY FRIENDS

If you're a reader, build a personal development library. Purchase the books, don't check them out of the library. You'll want to make notes in the margins of each book as the spirit moves you. Highlight significant passages. Underline powerful messages. Bracket important paragraphs. Star sentences which speak to you, deepen you, cause you to question encrusted beliefs or blind assumptions.

Revisit these paper gurus periodically. Re-read the highlighted parts. Review your notes. Underline new sections. Scribble more insights. Assess how you've changed, how much you've grown, how wise you've become.

You'll find you've out-grown some of these *literary friends* after a while. Or think you have. So add to your library, don't subtract, (unless you positively have to because of space limitations, economics or enlightenment.)

I hesitate to list a few of my *old friends* because the trip is different for each of us. Go to a bookstore and see which books choose you! These Literary Friends will lighten your load. So invest in yourself. If you're a reader, read to build a better you. If you're not a reader, now is a good time to become one.

GO TO SLEEP AND RISE & SHINE WITH INSPIRATION

Keep a book of quotes, spiritual guidance, short inspirational essays or poetry by your bedside, and read something positive right before you go to sleep. Upon awaking, grab the book and start your day with something uplifting and positive.

The best of a book is not the thought which it contains,
but the thought which it suggests.
                                    (Oliver Wendell Holmes)

ONE SHORT OF A HUNDRED

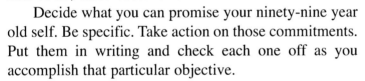

Imagine yourself as a fit, vibrant and healthy ninety-nine year old. Now, describe yourself. Yes, out loud. Boast a little. Brag if you must. What did you do note-worthy between ages twenty-five and ninety-nine? What are you doing now? Be specific. Now, write a letter *to yourself at your current age* **from** *you as a ninety-nine year old.* What would you tell yourself? What advice would you give yourself? What investments in time, money and friendships would you tell yourself to make? What goals would you suggest to your younger self? If there is one thing you'd want your younger self to be sure to do, what would it be?

Decide what you can promise your ninety-nine year old self. Be specific. Take action on those commitments. Put them in writing and check each one off as you accomplish that particular objective.

STOP WORRYING BY
MAKING IT COST YOU!

Worry is the most ineffective emotion we possess. Either you can do something about the problem — in which case you need to stop worrying and take action — or you can't do anything about it — in which case it does you no good to worry! Whenever you catch yourself worrying, charge yourself $5.00. Pretty soon you'll real-ize that you can't afford to worry!

WHAT DO THE DOCTORS SAY?

According to Dr. Robert S. Eliot (Clinical Professor of Medicine, University of Nebraska), the main predictors of destructive levels of stress are fear, uncertainty and doubt, together with perceived lack of control. Dr. Redford Williams, of Duke University Medical Center, says that hostility can create deterioration in the heart function of patients with a heart disease. He suggests changing your cynical thoughts into positive ones.

INDIANA JONES EXPERIENCES

Once every couple of months, do an activity you've never done before. Push your envelope. Stretch yourself. Move just a little out of your comfort zone. If you want, take some friends along with you.

I have found the following adventures to offer plenty of challenges: white water rafting, mountain climbing, fire walking, ropes challenge courses, spelunking, sky diving (or its' sister, parachuting), snorkeling, big-game hunting (with camera only), hang gliding, para-gliding.

Of course, you don't have to make it risky or life-threatening. Other kinds of unique Indiana Jones experiences could include: ballroom dancing, gourmet cooking, Velcro-wall jumping, horse-back riding, making pottery, oil painting, calligraphy, habitat for humanity involvement, attending a clown college or improvisational comedy course, hiking, water sports, photography, exercise and fitness activities, meditation, piecing together jig-saw puzzles, traveling somewhere you've never been, writing poetry or the great American novel, planting a tree or shrub or flowers and so on. The secret is to make it something you've never done before, and have some hesitancy about doing. You should feel just a little inner resistance.

Treat yourself to a sense of adventure. Leave your worries behind. Amaze yourself at what you can do. Don't take yourself too seriously. Your goal is to stretch yourself, expand your horizons, have fun, and move to a new level of awareness. Consult with your family doctor before you jump into some of these activities. And if you see Indiana Jones in your travels, tell him I said *hi*.

DEVELOP A FUN FILE

Make a list of things you enjoy doing, and post it where you can't miss seeing it. Make time each week to do something from that list. Keep a journal of memories related to your fun experiences.

INNER PEACE

Call Center Director: I've been to seminars and stress management workshops. I've read all the recommended self-improvement books. I've listened to motivational speakers who claimed to have the answers. I've done all of that. What I want to know is - where do you find inner peace?

Cher: *Where* is the wrong question! Inner peace isn't a place, so searching for it will continue to frustrate you. You can't find inner peace out there. You can't find it by looking for it. All you have to do is accept it. Claim it. Get out of your own way. Choose it. Say to yourself: *I am at peace.* Believe there is a part of you (for me, it is God) that's always in control. Know that there is a part of you that always has the answer. Trust the part of you which says: *It'll be all right. Be patient. Be still. Things have a way of working themselves out.*

RESTORE YOUR SOUL

When things feel out of control, make time to be apart from the madness. Go for a walk in the woods, sit by a gentle stream, stretch out in a hammock, listen to peaceful music, or take a hot bath. Do something that forces you to quiet yourself and listen to the peace within. I like to repeat the Bible verse from Psalms 23 that says "He restoreth my soul." During times of stress, we all need to claim opportunities to restore our soul.

PAMPER YOURSELF

Even if it's only for ten minutes, look for little things to do for yourself. Read a chapter in a good book; relax — guilt free; have a cup of herb tea or exotic coffee in a special mug; walk barefoot in the grass; do anything that makes you feel pampered, special and relaxed.

For peace of mind, resign as General Manager of the Universe!

EARLY YOUTH SNAPSHOTS

There is much to be learned from our early youth. Spend time alone or with a trusted friend filling in the blanks that apply to you. Enjoy the journey back to your early youth, and discover what lessons that part of your lifetime has to teach you.

Years 6 - 12

What I remember about my first year in school is ____
_____

My favorite teachers were _____
_____

I hated my _____ grade teacher because _____
_____

My favorite subjects were _____

_____

My feelings about homework were _____

_____

My best friends thought I was _____

_____

My favorite thing I did for fun was _____

_____

The biggest lesson I learned was _____

_____

I considered myself _____

_____

If I could have changed one thing about myself, it would
have been _____

_____

One thing my parents never found out was _____

_____

Every child is an artist. The problem is how to remain an
artist once he grows up.

(Picasso)

INNER SPACE

College Senior: How can I find peace with myself when
I'm so mixed up?

Cher: Start with the parts of you that are at peace. Use
them as anchors to keep you centered. Study the
chaotic you, the restless you, the unsure you. Pick one
thought, attitude or behavior that keeps you off balance. Mend it. Get help if you need it. Then focus on
another part of you that needs repair - or boundaries.
Add it to the part of you that is at peace. I know that's
a long answer to your question, but self-improvement
is about incremental improvement.

> **EMOTIONS INFLUENCE IMMUNITY:**
> Recent scientific evidence that lends support to a holistic view of the body is helping to move some mind-body therapies into the mainstream. Researchers have discovered that there is a continuous dialogue between the nervous, immune and endocrine systems, suggesting that emotions influence immunity — positive emotions may bolster it and negative emotions depress it.
> *The New York Times*, Oct. 4, 1992

DO WE NEED PLANNED SABBATICALS?

Computer Programmer: Are monastic periods, vision quests and sabbaticals necessary for achieving inner peace?

Cher: Only if you think they are.

It has always been interesting to me to observe that the only time...people will allow themselves the simple pleasure of relaxing in bed all day is when they are sick.

(Phil Lant)

TEEN-AGE SNAPSHOTS

Your teenage years have messages to share with you. Spend a little time reliving this period of your life, filling in the blanks that apply to you. Walk back into the past alone or with a friend. Have fun remembering the teenaged you.

Years 13 - 19

When I became thirteen, I _____

_____

My teen hangout was _____

My closest friend was _____

On my sixteenth birthday, I _____

My relationship to drugs and alcohol was _____

My favorite movie/TV stars were _____

Sex to me was _____

Getting my driver's license meant _____

The most important thing I learned from school was _____

High school graduation meant _____

What I learned about boy/girl relationships was _____

If I could do it over again, I would _____

When one is out of touch with oneself, one cannot touch others.

(Anne Morrow Lindbergh)

TALKING MYSELF OUT OF FRUSTRATION

I've had many opportunities to practice what I preach. Here's a powerful example of talking to yourself to relieve frustration and actually refocus your emotions. I was in Atlanta to conduct a two-day seminar for a client. In preparation for the session, I had been in com-

munication with my contact, and had received, among
other things, logistical data concerning where I would
stay and where the session would be held. My contact
actually faxed me specific directions to the Marriott,
indicating that I would be staying there and the session
would be held there. Imagine my dismay when, at
10:00 pm Sunday evening I arrived at the Marriott
(after a flight and long drive from the airport in my
rental car) to discover there was no room reservation
for me. To make matters worse, when I asked about
which room the session would be held in, they
informed me that there was no program scheduled for
that company. I showed them my faxed directions to
be sure I was in the correct location, and they agreed
that the directions were for their hotel, but nothing was
scheduled there.

As I pondered what to do (not having a home number of my contact — since this experience, I always
get one now), I became aware of a man registering in
the line next to me. He told the hotel clerk that he was
here for a seminar with my client company. I excitedly said, "Oh, good! Where is that seminar being held?
I'm supposed to teach it!" He said it was being held at
their corporate headquarters, about five miles away.
This calmed me down, I got a room and had a good
night's sleep, arose early and took off for the corporate
headquarters.

To make an extremely long, involved story a little
shorter, let me just say that the seminar the gentleman
at the hotel was in town for, was not the one I was to
teach. I was directed to two other facilities my client
had in the area before I found someone who knew
about my seminar. We finally discovered that I had
been faxed the directions to the wrong hotel, and I was
given directions to get to where my seminar (and my

client contact — who was frantically wondering where I was) was waiting. Those directions were a bit messed up also, and I found myself driving around Atlanta in rush hour traffic, trying to find the hotel where my seminar was being held. The more I drove, the more upset I became. Then I started the process of talking to myself, saying: *Cher, you're doing the best you can. You are going to get there when you get there. You can't get there any sooner. Just stay calm, and find the humor in this whole mix-up!* Believe it or not, I became calm. I visualized my client laughing about the situation, and saw it creating a great story. I saw myself in control — and arriving in good form to conduct the class. Sure enough, when I walked in — 30 minutes after scheduled start-up time, my client contact was embarrassed, admitted her error, and wanted to do anything at all to make me feel good about the situation. It became a focal point for jokes during the class, and it built great rapport. However, and here's my point, had I allowed myself to become all upset, I would have gotten angry, said things to my client contact that would have created negative emotions, and I never would have been able to walk in and immediately begin to teach a two-day session. This stuff really works — I promise!

The ability to laugh at life is right at the top of our hierarchy of needs.

Make a **Humor Bulletin Board** designed for appropriate cartoons, quotes, pictures and write ups of funny things that have happened.

VISUALIZE WHAT YOU WANT

Learn to use the power of visualization to help you claim positive mental as well as physical health. Research confirms that the mind does not know the difference between fantasy and reality, so feed it the images you want to see materialized in your life.

HOW DO YOU VISUALIZE?

One reason a lot of people resist using visualization is because they aren't clear about what it is. We talk about it, but fail to mention that different people use their imagination in different ways. Let me show you in 5 quick seconds exactly how you imagine — then you can begin to consciously use your power to create your good. Imagine for a moment that I am a window washer (this is definitely a stretch, but we're imagining, right?)! I am coming to your house this weekend to wash your windows. (Don't get excited — this is just imagination — I'm not really coming!) All I need is for you to think for a moment, and tell me exactly how many windows you have in your house.

What are you doing right now? I bet you are counting windows! However you are doing it is how you imagine! For example, some folks close their eyes and actually SEE their house. In my programs, I can see their heads bob up and down as they literally move through their home, counting windows as they go. Others kind of talk to themselves: "I have three in the living room, and two in the kitchen . . . " Still others are more kinesthetic, and appear to be touching windows with their fingers as they count in their mind. The important factor to recognize here is that NOT EVERYONE ACTUALLY SEES PICTURES IN THEIR MIND! Many people have a more intuitive sense of what they are imagining, rather than an actual picture. There is no right or wrong. It is simply your preferred style. Use it for your benefit!

NORMAN VINCENT PEALE'S LESSON ON THE POWER OF VISUALIZATION

In his book *Positive Imaging*, Norman Vincent Peale shares a story of his discovery of the power of imaging that astounded me. He and his wife, Ruth, started a magazine that you may be familiar with - Guideposts. (If you're not familiar with it, I strongly suggest you get your hands on a copy. It is filled with truly inspiring stories of real people, and real experiences). The Peales started this magazine with only $700 in working capital. Its subscription list had risen to approximately 40,000, but financially the situation was disastrous. Cash flow was nonexistent and the very future of the magazine was in jeopardy.

Peale shares that the directors held a meeting to discuss the sad state of affairs. Present at that meeting was a wonderful lady named Tessie Durlack, who had previously made a generous contribution. Peale admitted that he secretly hoped she would come through with another donation to help them out of their financial jam. But she didn't. Instead she stated, "I'm going to give you folks something far more valuable than money — an idea which will lead to your prosperity. You have been imagining lack, and have therefore created lack — in everything: subscribers, equipment, capital. Now you must start imaging prosperity instead!"

You can imagine the response! There was considerable doubt about the impact of thoughts on reality. Tessie boldly quoted Plato: Take charge of your thoughts. You can do what you will with them.

She went on to describe the technique of visualizing, and led this group of doubting directors through an exercise of visualizing one hundred thousand persons as subscribers to Guideposts, all of whom had paid for their subscriptions. She then thanked the Lord for providing the subscribers.

Peale emphasizes that the stack of unpaid bills did not miraculously disappear. But what did happen was that the directors, previously discouraged and down-hearted, suddenly came alive, and began to generate creative ideas. Subscriptions poured in, and today Guideposts has 3,600,000 subscribers, is read monthly by 12 million persons, and is the 14th largest magazine in the U.S.

The mind is a strange machine which can combine the materials offered to it in the most astonishing way.

(Bertrand Russell)

EARLY ADULTHOOD SNAPSHOTS

Who were you in your twenties and thirties? What did you do? What lessons does this period of your life have to teach you? Complete the blanks that apply to you, alone or with a significant other.

Years 20 - 39

I generally thought of myself as _____

_____

When I was in school I was glad I _____

_____

When I was in school, I wish I had _____

_____

For me, drugs and alcohol were _____

_____

For the first time, I understood what my parents meant when they _____

_____

My closest friends were _____

_____

In regard to a career, I always wanted to be _____
_____

The hardest thing for me to do was _____
_____

Work for me was _____
Marriage was _____
My view of success then, was _____
_____

If I could have changed one thing about myself, it would
have been _____
_____

When we cannot find contentment in ourselves, it is use-
less to seek it elsewhere.
(Francois de La Rochefoucauld)

YOUR DREAM SCREEN

The Dream Screen requires you to spend a little time alone, where you can get quiet and not be interrupted. Take a few deep breaths to relax yourself, and close your eyes. Now, imagine a blank screen in your mind. Think about how you feel in a movie theater, just as the lights dim but before a picture comes on the screen. You are staring at a blank screen, in anticipation of what is to come. Transfer that feeling to your mind. Now, on that screen play out your dream — your goal — your desire. Create it just the way you would like it to be. Hear the words being said; imagine the feelings being generated; see the surroundings, the expressions, the colors. Make this movie as vivid and real as you possibly can. Remember, you are the director of this show!

PROOF FOR THE DIEHARDS: One final study, for those of you who are diehard research buffs and want real proof! Researchers at Washington State University investigated whether visualization techniques could reduce "communication apprehension," the discomfort some people feel when faced with public speaking. They studied 107 students in a public-speaking class who experienced this fear. The students were divided into four groups. One group practiced a visualization technique during the week before giving a speech. They were coached to imagine the best possible scenario for the entire day of the speech: putting on just the right clothes; feeling clear, confident and thoroughly prepared; giving a smooth, brilliant speech that was well received. A control group was given no training at all. The two remaining groups were taught commonly-used confidence building methods: muscle relaxation for one group and rational-thinking techniques for the other. The students who used visualization had significantly lower scores on a test of communication apprehension than students in any of the other three groups.

NOSE JOB OR HEAD JOB?

Consider the story shared by Maxwell Maltz, a plastic surgeon. A young salesman who was about to quit his job consulted Dr. Maltz about performing surgery on his nose. He insisted that his nose was repulsive, prospects were secretly laughing behind his back at his nose, and as a result he was not effective in sales. This surgery was a last resort before quitting for good. Dr. Maltz analyzed the actual facts in the case. It was a fact that the salesman did, indeed, have a nose that was slightly larger than normal. It was a fact that three customers had called in to complain of his rude and hostile behavior. It was a fact that his boss had placed him on probation, and that he hadn't made a sale in two weeks.

Instead of a nose operation, Dr. Maltz suggested to this patient that he perform surgery on his own thinking. They made a deal. For 30 days, the salesman agreed to cut out all the negative thoughts. He was to ignore all the negative and unpleasant facts in his situation, and instead focus on pleasant thoughts. Every day he was to visualize himself as successful and effective as a sales-man, and visualize his prospects in positive ways. If, after 30 days he still wanted nose surgery, Dr. Maltz agreed he would do it.

At the end of the 30-day period, this salesman not only felt much better; he found his prospects and cus-tomers were "transformed" into more friendly individuals, and his sales were increasing. In fact, he had been publicly recognized by his boss in a sales meeting. Needless to say, no nose surgery was necessary (from *Psycho-Cybernetics*, Maxwell Maltz).

One of the most important things in life is the need not to accept downside predictions from experts. No one knows enough to make a pronouncement of doom.
(Norman Cousins)

MIRROR, MIRROR ON THE WALL

When you look at yourself in a mirror, who do you see? What kind of person are you? How healthy are you? How well do you look? Are you happy? What would you change about yourself? Say something meaningful to yourself.

CREATE A DREAMSCAPE

This tool comes from the idea of landscaping. I have a friend who has his own landscaping business, and he shared with me the process he goes through when designing someone's yard. It's quite an involved process, which I won't go into with detail here. The one step I want to emphasize is the Landscape Blueprint. This professional draws on paper a blueprint of the customer's yard, and then literally plants the shrubbery and foliage on paper. When he is done, you can look at his beautiful, colorized, detailed drawing and see immediately how the finished product will look. Even if it is a process that will take years to finalize, you carry that finished product in your mind, and you realize that every step is leading you to that final result.

This led me to the idea of creating a Dreamscape. With a dreamscape, as with a landscape blueprint, you take an inner idea and manifest it into an outer reality. I affectionately call this strategy Cut and Paste 101. You are literally cutting out actual pictures, words and images and pasting them onto tag board, creating a visual picture of your goals and desires. Keep your Dreamscape where you can see it daily, and imprint your goals in your mind and consciousness.

DREAMING OF A BUSINESS

One of my very first attempts at the idea of dream-scaping was when Bil and I decided we really wanted to have our own consulting business. We cut out words and designed a notebook cover that looked like workshop materials for one of our programs. Then we got all dressed up in business suits, and had a friend take our picture holding this notebook. We kept that picture on our refrigerator for 2 years — and here we are! We've had our own business since 1983 — and love it! Of course, it took more than a picture on a refrigerator to make it happen, but that picture kept the image in our minds, and reminded us that every step we took was leading us to that goal.

DREAMSCAPING A WEIGHT CHANGE

Here is another success example, just to demonstrate the wide variety of ways Dreamscaping works. I discovered that I had, during a ten year period, slowly but quite definitely added about 20 extra pounds to my body. It happened so gradually that I hadn't really been aware of it, until all of a sudden, one day, I woke up and found out I had a weight problem to deal with. (Actually, I thought the Dry Cleaners and my dryer were shrinking my clothes!)

In various magazines I identified photos of women with a similar body type to mine (but in fantastic shape!), and cut them out. I then cut off their heads, and replaced them with my head (cut from various photos). The effect was phenomenal! Here were these fabulous bodies, all looking like me! What a great way to convince myself that I truly could look like that. Some of the pictures were of women exercising and working out. I included lots of encouraging words and phrases (The Perfect Body Image; New Body; Slimmer), and spiritual symbols to ensure Divine Order. With the help of Weight Watchers I lost nearly 30 pounds, and feel better than I ever have in my life! Maintenance has been fairly easy, because, you see, I didn't go on a diet. I changed my lifestyle, and brought my mental picture of myself in line with what I desired. I still have that Dreamscape as a powerful reminder of the importance of maintaining a healthy, fit body.

Weight Loss Research: According to experts, people who lose weight, then gain it back again do so because they fail to have a clear picture of themselves at their new weight. When they see themselves in the mirror, they literally still see themselves at their heavier weight. They then eat their way back to a weight that is consistent with their image.

 Happiness lies in the joy of achievement and the thrill of creative effort.

(Franklin Roosevelt)

MID-LIFE SNAPSHOTS

 If you've experienced life in the 40-60 age range, looking back can evoke some interesting memories. . . and some valuable lessons to help you as you journey into your future. Complete each of these statements that apply to you honestly and thoughtfully. Enjoy your trip.

Years 40 - 60

Work for me was _____

_____

My married life was _____

_____

What I discovered about myself was _____

_____

I found that I had to _____

_____

My health was _____

_____

My parents were _____

_____

My favorite car (truck, utility vehicle) was _____

_____

Despite my best intentions the one habit I couldn't seem to break was _____

_____

My basic philosophy of life was _____

_____

The biggest mistake I made was _____

_____

I wish I had _____

_____

The career I wanted was _____

_____

Financially, I _____

_____

Exercise for me was _____

_____

My greatest disappointment was _____

_____

The things I was most proud of were _____

_____

One important lesson I learned was _____

_____

Thinking is the talking of the soul with itself.

(Plato)

STOP PLAYING THE WHEN/THEN GAME

The "When/Then" Game goes like this: A little baby in the crib observes the activity going on around him — just beyond his bars. If we could read his mind, we'd hear him thinking, "Boy! **When** I get out of here and walk, **then** I'll be happy! That's all I need — just to be able to walk!"

Let's follow this little fellow as he takes his first tottering steps…and then learns to walk. As he explores the environment, he notices his older sister going off to school. Now he's thinking, "Boy, If I could just be old enough to go to school. I want to get out of this place — into the world. **When** I can go to school, **then** I'll be happy."

Moving ahead a few years at a time, we now hear this little guy's thoughts verbalized. At different stages, you'll hear: "Boy, **when** I get those Reeboks Pump Shoes, **then** I'll be happy!" "**When** I get on the basketball team, **then** I'll be happy." "**When** I get my driver's license, **then** I'll be happy." "**When** I graduate and get a job, **then** I'll be happy." "**When** I meet that perfect mate, **then** I'll be happy." "**When** we get married, **then** I'll be happy." "**When** we can buy a house, **then** I'll be happy." "**When** we have our children, **then** I'll be happy." "**When** these kids are out of the house, **then** I'll be happy." "**When** I get that promotion, **then** I'll be happy." "**When** I retire, **then** I'll be happy." And then he dies…still pursuing the happiness he could never quite claim as his own . . . an ultimate loser in the game of When/Then in Life. A sad scenario — and much too common.

Get out of the When/Then Game, and start playing the I'm Happy Now Because Game. Look at where you are right now, in this moment, and appreciate your strengths, your accomplishments and your successes.

One of the most tragic things I know about human nature is that all of us tend to put off living. We are all dreaming of some magical rose garden over the horizon — instead of enjoying the roses that are blooming outside our windows today.

(Dale Carnegie)

MAKE IT OKAY

Part of releasing the pursuit of happiness means releasing forever the belief that your happiness depends on someone else's actions. In his wonderful book *Illusions*, Richard Bach says, "If your happiness depends on what somebody else does…you do have a problem." One of my favorite phrases is "Make it O.K." I remember when I had a challenge with a colleague. I'd sent a letter apologizing for any misunderstanding that had occurred and was anxiously awaiting a reply. Bil asked me how I'd feel if this colleague remained upset about the situation. Would my happiness depend on his reaction — or could I feel good about my response and release the whole situation? That was my first conscious decision to "Make it O. K." for my colleague to remain upset if he so chose. Since then, that little phrase has released a lot of pressure in potentially stressful situations. And, by the way, my colleague reacted very favorably to my letter, and things turned out fine. Thank goodness I didn't waste my energy with worry about it.

LEARN FROM THE PAST

Take a moment to go into the recesses of your memory, and identify a situation from your past when something was not going well. It may be a past emotional experience, or a health challenge, or perhaps a financial disaster — some time when you felt things were awful, and you felt you didn't want to go on. Be sure it is something from your past that has since been resolved, not something you're dealing with right now.

Got a handle on a specific experience? Now, looking at it from the perspective of today, can you identify at least one lesson you learned from it, or one result from it, that made it worth while? Identify something that occurred that allows you to honestly say, "I wouldn't want to go through that again, but because of this, I'm actually glad it happened."

What a comforting realization, knowing that no matter how tough the road, there is always some good that can come, if we will allow it.

Remember: The darkest hour has only 60 minutes.

BEYOND 60 SNAPSHOTS

If you are over 60, you know that life continues to provide lessons that contribute to your inner peace — if only you pay attention. Take some time to think about what you've learned since you passed that 60 mark, and complete the following statements that apply to you.

Years 60 and beyond

I'm perfectly satisfied with _____

_____

I find I can no longer _____

_____

One of my favorite pastimes is _____

_____

For me, sex is now _____

_____

My favorite TV show is _____

_____

I particularly like to read _____

_____

If I have any regrets _____

_____

My favorite physical activity is _____

_____

I'm finally at peace with   _____

_____

The thing I wish I had done more of is _____

_____

The best advice I can give to young people is   _____

_____

My favorite photo of the family is _____

_____

The three things I enjoy most about life are   _____

_____

Looking back at my life, I've learned that _____

_____

Though we travel the world over to find the beautiful, we must carry it with us or we find it not.
(Ralph Waldo Emerson)

ALL OF THEM COUNT

Realtor: You talk about the power of choice, but do our choices in simple things really make that much difference?

Cher: Let's put it this way. We make thousands of choices every day, both consciously and unconsciously. Every choice contributes to your overall life experience. I believe you cannot manage your life unless you manage your choices. And you cannot manage your choices unless you manage yourself. This means you must become consciously aware of the impact of every choice you make, and recognize the amount of power you really do have.

CLEAR A SPACE

Clear a space in your heart for love… compassion… forgiveness. List twelve things you love. Twelve ways you have shown compassion. Twelve things you have forgiven yourself or others for. Once you clear a space in your heart, you clear a space in your life that repels fear and doubt and loneliness. Your inner voice, your soul's voice, ventures into the clearing you have uncluttered for it. Review the list of the twelve things you love. Experience several of them again, healthily and happily.

THIRTY DAYS

Write "I am wise, well and happy" on a sheet of paper thirty times a day for the next thirty days. Say it to yourself as often as you can over the same time period. Both of these activities will help you balance your internal ledger.

The quieter you become, the more you can hear
(Baba Ram Dass)

COMMUNICATING
EFFECTIVELY

COMMUNICATING EFFECTIVELY — SNEAK PEEK

Mark Twain once said that the difference between the right word and the almost right word is the difference between lightning and the lightning bug. That sums up the power of effective communication versus almost effective communication. My experience validates that at least 80% of the problems with relationships, with productivity, with quality, with customers, with business growth, with safety — literally, with every experience we encounter — comes back to a problem with communication. Somebody misunderstood, shared wrong information, withheld information, or misinterpreted the meaning of what was communicated. And these days, there are so many forms of communication to deal with. We not only have face-to-face contacts . . . which involve the power of nonverbal communication and the impact of tone of voice; we also have telephone, voice mail, email, faxes, pagers, and snailmail.

Communication is defined by Webster as a "process by which meanings are exchanged between individuals." It is the key ingredient in all good business and interpersonal relationships. Whenever we are with people, we communicate in some manner - and usually in more ways than one.

Although we communicate in words, we communicate equally by our tone of voice, our facial expressions, our body movements, our apparel, the company we keep, and the environment we create around ourselves. Silence itself is a form of communication.

Communication fails, unnecessarily, when we assume that the meaning behind our words can be poured into another individual's mind like pouring water into a glass. The same statement may have an entirely different meaning to two people. Individual differences in temperament, education, values, beliefs and experience are vital factors in the communication process. We must also control the rate and amount of information we communicate — too much information can create information overload, causing an individual's head to spin.

Communication is a **means,** not an end. It is the means through which planning is performed, problems are resolved, relationships are built, emotions are tamed and information is shared. In this important section, discover ways to take responsibility for the communication situations in which you find yourself. You'll find tips to help you with verbal and nonverbal communication; even telephone, email and fax communications. The strategies will work in both personal and work settings.

No matter where you are, you cannot control what another person says, but more than you can imagine, you CAN control the situation when it is your turn to speak. To a great degree, your success is determined by your skill in communication competence. Better communication can lead to more effective performance (which can make your *job* a lot easier) and improved interpersonal relationships (which can make your *life* a lot easier).

The privilege and the power of building our communication excellence is best summed up by Daniel Webster's quote: "If all my talents and powers were to be taken from me by some inscrutable Providence, and I had my choice of keeping but one, I would unhesitatingly ask to be allowed to keep the power of Speaking, for through it, I would quickly recover all the rest."

THE LADDER TOWARD IMPROVED COMMUNICATIONS

This tool is invaluable in helping you improve the outcomes of your communication experiences. It forces you to take responsibility for what is happening, and reframe what the other person is saying. It's not for the faint-hearted, but it brings fabulous results.

Think back over some of your biggest communication fiascoes. How many were the result of over-reacting to something someone did or said; making broad generalizations based on stereotypes; misinterpreting a behavior and responding inappropriately? By using the Ladder Technique, you can reflect on what actually is happening in a communication.

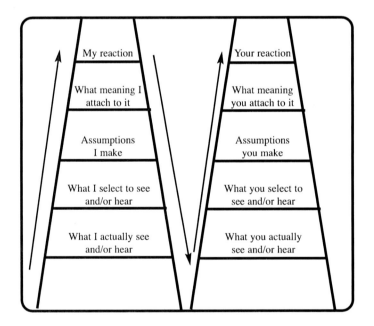

We move up and down this ladder in steps, and the entire climb happens in a split second as we progress through a communication encounter. Here's what happens:

Step 1: We actually hear and/or see something. This is the "fact" stage. It is specific and tangible. But we quickly take a big step up to the next rung.

Step 2: We *select* what we choose to focus on. Everyone practices 'selective listening' and 'selective vision'. We choose to focus on the part(s) of the situation that catch our attention. Then we quickly move to the next rung of the ladder.

Step 3: We make assumptions about what we have selected to focus on. Based on our background, values, experiences and attitudes, we jump to conclusions about what we've heard. As a result of that, we jump a rung up.

Step 4: We attach meaning to those assumptions. This takes us up to that top rung.

Step 5: We react! This entire climb up the ladder happens in a split second, and as soon as we react, the other person begins their ladder climb!

Here are six specific strategies to improve your ladder climbing:

- Reflect on your own thinking and reasoning process.
- Clarify the observable data — what are the facts?
- Share your interpretations with others, explaining your thought process.
- Inquire into the meaning intended by others. ("When you said _____, what exactly did you mean?" or "I'm thinking you're saying _____. Am I on track?")
- Test your assumptions!!
- Give other people the benefit of a doubt!

Lawyers insist that the least accurate — although often the most persuasive — evidence is that of an eyewitness.

 *There's something exhilarating about showing other people the links of your reasoning. They may or may not agree with you, but they can see how you got there. And you're often surprised yourself to see how you got there, once you trace out the links.*

(Rick Ross)

EMBARRASSING CLIMB UP THE LADDER

On one of our vacations, we included a visit to Fort McHenry, in Baltimore, MD. We began our visit by attending the informative film, introducing us to the history of the site. During the film, two people behind me were talking in a loud whisper. The longer the film went, the more they whispered.

I could not imagine why these people were being so rude and inconsiderate. My thinking was: "If they didn't want to see the film, why not wait outside?" Their voices became so annoying to me I found I could not even pay attention to the film. I glanced around a few times with a glare, hoping that would be enough to silence them. No such luck. Finally I turned around and said, "Shh-shh," then huffily turned back to the film.

A moment later, the woman behind me leaned forward, gently touched my shoulder and whispered, "I'm so sorry. He's visiting from Spain, and doesn't understand English. I was trying to interpret what was happening to him. We'll try to do it more quietly."

Wham! Did I feel stupid and rude. I immediately apologized for my rudeness, then settled back to enjoy the rest of the film. Interestingly enough, the soft murmur of voices behind me no longer bothered me at all. And after the film, Bil and I had a nice visit with those wonderful people behind us, discovering how someone from Spain was enjoying his visit to our country.

Once a human being has arrived on...earth, communi-cation is the largest single factor determining what kinds of relationships he makes with others and what happens to him ... How he manages his survival, how he devel-ops intimacy, how productive he is, how he makes sense ... are largely dependent on his communication skills.

(V. Satir)

THE POWER OF "KNOW"

Look at the word written below, and say it out loud:

NO

Say it again...and again. There! You've proven you *can* say NO. So you can no longer use the excuse "I just can't say NO!"

Now, say the word written below:

KNOW

Say it again. Do you realize these two words sound the same? So if you have trouble saying NO, just say KNOW. People will think you're saying NO!

Seriously, there is a very important principle at work here: ***If you KNOW why you want or need to say NO, it's a whole lot easier to say it.*** In other words, if you have your priorities in order, have clarified your goals and understand your values, you know when requests by others are pulling you off track. To put it another way, *those who do not have their goals and priorities in order are used by those who do!* So recognize the Power of KNOW.

PRACTICE SAYING NO

We were having dinner one evening with friends, when their telephone rang. Bernie got up and answered it, while the rest of us sat at the table, overhearing his

side of the conversation. After his initial hello, there was a pause. Then Bernie yelled into the phone: "NO! Absolutely not! Don't call again!"

This absolutely floored the rest of us, because Bernie is a quiet, kind, thoughtful man (a little too kind, sometimes!). We were staring at each other as he walked back into the room with a little smug smile on his face. He looked at us, then said, "That was Bob, the computer! I was practicing saying no!" His next lesson will be tact!

TIPS TO HELP YOU SAY "NO"

It isn't always easy to say no. Here are a few tools to help you as you build your skill in communicating a negative response to someone's request.

- *Give yourself time to say no.* Don't give an answer immediately. When someone asks you to do something, respond by saying "I'll need to check my calendar first. Let me get back to you with an answer." This gives you time to think through whether or not you want to do it, and if not, allows you to plan your answer.
- *Develop 'canned responses' for your most obvious situations.* We all have our Achilles heel — the situation in which we have the most difficulty saying no. Identify your weak spot and have a response all ready to use.
- *Practice saying "no" in non-threatening situations.* Practice your ability to say no when it doesn't matter. For example, say no when a salesperson asks you to take a sample of something; say no in the restaurant when the waitperson wants to bring a dessert tray; say no to the solicitor on the telephone. Each successful experience builds your confidence in your ability and your assertiveness.

SAY "BECAUSE . . ."

In a research experiment, people asked to break into line at a copier machine. In situation A, the person simply said, "Can I break in front of you?" The individual was allowed to break into line 26% of the time. In situation B, the individual said, "May I break in front of you, because I have to run these copies for a meeting starting in ten minutes?" The individual was permitted to break line 87% of the time. In situation C, the individual simply said, "Can I break in front of you because I need to make copies?" This individual was allowed to break line 86% of the time! The researchers determined that after hearing the word "because," people assume there is a good reason and stop listening.

One "NO" averts seventy evils.

(Indian Proverb)

THE POWER OF A 'CANNED RESPONSE'

One of my "saying no" challenges involved situations when I was at an out of town client site. Often, they felt a need to entertain me with a huge meal in the evening. I personally don't like to be out late, and the last thing I needed was a lot of rich food. But of course, I didn't want to offend my client by refusing. I came up with a 'canned response' to use whenever the situation occurred. When asked if they could take me out for a night on the town, I'd look right in their eye, smile and say, "I would love to go out for dinner with you, on two conditions. I'd like to go somewhere I can get something light, like salad and soup, and I really need to be back in my room by 8:00 so I can do my last minute preparations and get lots of rest so I can give you a dynamite program tomorrow!"

Guess what? Usually my client was as thrilled as I was. They didn't really want that late night eating out either! They were just trying to be nice to me!

MAKE YOUR 'NO' A 'YES'

Rather than just saying no, which can upset people, find a way to turn it into a positive. For example, instead of "No, I can't do that," you could say "I would love to do that, if you can move the date to _____." Other examples: "I really appreciate being considered for this, but I believe someone else should have the opportunity this year. Why don't you consider (and offer a few names)?" "Yes, I can do that, under these conditions . . . "

DEALING WITH 'NO'

If you're on the receiving end of a "no," be understanding of that person's need to turn down your request. Instead of harping on their rejection, or whining, or worse yet, begging them to change their mind, simply acknowledge their response. Then ask if they know anyone they would recommend who could do it instead. They are usually so joyful that you accepted their "no," they are delighted to help you find someone else.

BLACK & WHITE AND READ ALL OVER

Remember the old riddle: what's black and white and "red" (read) all over? The newspaper! Make one of your communication goals to be "read all over." Communicate with some of the best minds in the world! Read books of socially redeeming value. Digest them. Use them as inspirational tools. Make them your constant literary companions, your confidants, your personal gurus. Learn from other people's mistakes on paper. Avoid repeating them yourself. Build a personal library of self-help and inspirational texts. Study self-improvement books. Pour all of this knowledge into the pages of your own life on a daily basis. You'll be transformed. Some people might call it indoctrination or propaganda. But it's good indoctrination. It will put you in touch with yourself.

NAME CALLING

Secretary: People tell me I'm a workaholic. They say I'm a technocrat. Sometimes they call me a brownnoser. How can I deal with this?

Cher: Remember that old adage 'Sticks and stones can break my bones, but names can never hurt me'? Well, names may not break bones, but they *can* hurt — emotionally. Labels can be used for clarification or manipulation. The key is to decide for yourself who you are. Wear the label if it fits. Use diplomacy if it doesn't. But for heaven's sake, don't own it if you know it doesn't apply to you.

It's also helpful to realize that people throw out labels as a way to justify their own inadequacies or jealousies. I find that when someone hurls a label like 'workaholic' at me, the best thing to do is smile and say "Thank you!"

Labels can be linguistic handcuffs, but you have the key.
(Bil Holton)

CHILDHOOD WISDOM: I remember a saying from my childhood, when someone would use name calling to hurt me. I'd reply with "I'm rubber, you're glue. Whatever you call me bounces off me and sticks to you!"

BE CAREFUL OF INTERPRETATIONS

Nonverbal communication competence is a language which can speak louder than words. Sometimes nonverbal messages can scream out at you as you respond to another person's physical, psychological and emotional needs. Interpreting nonverbal behavior is just like interpreting the spoken word — neither should be taken out of context and the meanings attributed to each should be defined by the individual. Test your assumptions!

QUESTIONABLE RESEARCH, BUT WORTH CONSIDERING: Research by Albert Mehrabian indicates that 55% of the meaning another person gets from your communication comes from nonverbal; 38% from tone of voice; and 7% from the actual words being used. While this research has come under a lot of criticism and misinterpretation, the message is still worth considering. Pay attention to the nonverbal messages you are sending that may be in conflict with your words. My own research with clients takes these stats a step further. When you are on the telephone, the meaning derived from nonverbal is 0%; tone of voice jumps to 75-80%; and the impact of words increases to 20-25%.

He speaketh not; and yet there lies a conversation in his eyes.

(Henry Wadsworth Longfellow)

NONVERBALS ON THE TELEPHONE

Although it is true that nonverbals cannot be seen when you are on the phone, keep in mind that they still affect your tone of voice. That's why it's so important to smile when you answer the telephone! If you doubt the impact of nonverbals on tone, try saying "How may I help you?" in a pleasant way with a nasty expression on your face. You'll get the point!

EMAIL ETIQUETTE

While email makes it easier and faster to communicate with others, it has brought with it a host of new problems. Anyone who has opened their email to see or hear the words "You have 73 messages!" can appreciate what I mean. Here is some email etiquette — rules to help make email a help rather than a hindrance.

- Keep email messages short and to the point.
- Be clear about your expectation in terms of a response.
- Don't write anything you wouldn't be willing to have posted on the cafeteria wall of your workplace. Nothing is private!
- If you are angry when you write an email, save it for 24 hours and re-read it before you send it. (This applies to anything you write in anger!)
- Think twice, then think again before you mass-forward a joke, virus warning or other type of message.
- Verify any information before you forward it. Most virus warnings are pranks. There is just as much, if not more, junk coming through your computer as coming in your mail.
- Remember that people cannot hear your voice inflections in an email.
- Be considerate of other people's time.
- Remember: You don't have to respond to something just because someone asked you through email (unless, of course, it came from your manager!)

A TEST OF FRIENDSHIP

If you find you can't be with someone unless you're doing something together — skating, going to a play, in other words, a third thing to which you both direct your attention — then that person may not be as good a friend as you think. The real test of friendship is: can you literally do nothing with that person? Can you enjoy together those moments of life that are utterly simple? They are the moments that people look back on at the end of life and number as their most sacred experiences. (Eugene Kennedy)

IN THE BLINK OF AN EYE

Sales Rep: My manager blinks his eyes a lot. Isn't that a sign of nervousness?

Cher: Most researchers feel that excessive blinking indicates anxiety or certain kinds of nervousness … as if the blinking keeps reality at bay. There is some evidence suggesting that people who blink up to one hundred times per minute are extremely anxious, bordering on neurotic.

Sales Rep: What is the normal blinking rate?

Cher: Six to ten times per minute for adults. Blinking lubricates and protects the eyeball. But excessive blinking protects vulnerable egos.

Sales Rep: Is excessive blinking treatable?

Cher: It's as treatable as hypertension, nervousness, anxiety, deception and deceit. Treat the source of the nervousness and you treat the symptom…the blinking.

It is the nature of human communication to be incomplete … we can't say everything about anything. We can, however, strive to increase the precision, accuracy and relevance of what we do say.

(Mark Knapp)

WHAT ARE YOUR EYES SAYING?

Wide eyes may be associated with frankness, wonder, naiveté, or terror; downward glances with modesty; raised upper eyelids with displeasure. Constant stares are associated with coldness; eyes rolled upward can indicate fatigue or may suggest irritation and frustration with what someone else is saying or doing. (Research conducted by Mark Knapp)

The popular assumption that facial expressions are the universal language turns out to be not such a good call. They can cause huge misunderstandings between cultures, according to research studies. When shown photographs of expressions that virtually all Americans recognize in the same way, a group of 123 Japanese medical students almost all interpreted the emotions behind the expressions differently from the Americans.

(Los Angeles Times, 1/29/98)

GET A GRIP

Handshakes are an extremely powerful nonverbal tool, so be sure you 'get a grip' on what your handshake is communicating. The ideal handshake occurs when one person's hand fits into the other person's hand, with the area between the thumb and index finger connecting. There should be a gentle pressure, accompanied by two or three shakes while making eye contact and smiling; then, release hands.

Avoid the dead fish handshake, where one person's hand just lies in the other's, with no pressure. It implies you do not care and have a cold personality. Also avoid grabbing the ends of the fingers of the other person. This leaves them feeling demeaned and a little irritated. And watch out for the bone cruncher, that squeezes all the life out of the other person's hand and brings them to their knees. This is not a strength contest!

KEEP OUT

Magazine Editor: Our offices — or should I say cubicles — are getting smaller and smaller. Why does it feel like I'm more protective than ever of the tiny space that's "mine?"

Cher: What you're describing is a concept called territoriality. It refers to behavior characterized by emotional identification with a specific area or location in such a way that indicates ownership. The person is over-protective of the territory and is defensive if the territory is *invaded*. With our downsized environment, people want to claim what little space they have and protect it.

  As a matter of fact there are, generally speaking, three types of territories: primary, secondary and public. Primary territories are the exclusive domain of the owner . . . Like someone's cubicle at work . . . or even a room in the home like the bedroom or the study. Personal effects, like wallets, purses, sweaters or rings also qualify as primary territorial items.

Magazine Editor: What about things like the TV, books, staplers? Or my scissors, which keep sprouting legs and walking off my desk?

Cher: Those are known as secondary territories. They are not as valued or central to the daily life of the owner. People feel more comfortable "borrowing" these items, since they aren't as personal. Places like storage rooms, break-out areas, lunch rooms, or shop floors are also considered secondary territories, since they are shared by a group of people with common bonds of some type.

Magazine Editor: And public territories?

Cher: Libraries, training rooms, beaches, streets and sidewalks, and restaurants would all be examples of public territories. So would items such as pay telephones, magazines in the reception areas, or condiments at a fast-food restaurant. Ownership of these territories is shared by individuals with no common bonds. Possession is usually temporary, for a specific purpose. And getting people to take responsibility for areas gets more difficult as you move from personal through to public.

DRESS FOR SUCCESS

Dressing for success used to be fairly easy. There were rules that made sense, and were universally accepted throughout the business world. Not so any more. With the advent of "business casual," dressing for work has become a nightmare!

A basic rule of thumb: Dress for the position you want, not necessarily the position you currently possess.

A Corollary: Choose clothing that is appropriate for the situation, and at the same time projects the best image possible.

CLOTHESHORSE OR PURPOSEFUL CHAMELEON?

Boeing chairman and chief executive Phil Condit changes his clothes two or three times a day at the office, slipping in and out of sweaters, suits and sport coats. Since he began allowing casual dress five days a week, he needs clothes on hand to present an appropriate image when meeting with customers, as well as meeting with employees.

Not only do employees now have to spend thousands on a new wardrobe to deal with "business casual"; they have to be on guard for dress culture clashes! One executive admitted that he calls ahead and asks secretaries to clue him in on the dress code before he visits a client site. (*Associated Press*)

POLL TO DETERMINE BUSINESS DRESS CODE

According to a survey [funded by Levi Strauss & Co.] of 900 workers, more than half of white-collar employees can now dress casually every day, compared with 33% two years ago.

Clothing power should not be underestimated. What you wear is an important part of who you are. At first glance, no one knows what you're like on the inside — it is the outer packaging that draws others to you.

(Joanne Wallace)

BODYWORKS RESEARCH

- Most American men and women dress for failure. (Molloy)
- Pedestrians will violate the instructions given by a traffic signal more often when another person violates it ahead of them. There were significantly more violations when the original violator was dressed to represent a high status person. (Mefkowitz, Blake, Mouton)
- People who wear eyeglasses are generally considered higher in intelligence and industriousness. (Thornton)
- Attractive men and women are more likely to be helped and less likely to be the objects of aggressive acts. (Berscheid, Walster)
- Non-verbal indicators of high status include: clothing ornamentation with power symbols; greater physical height; gray-pin-striped business suits; greater territorial access; and more frequent use of arms akimbo. (Mehrabian)
- Individuals perceived as attractive, competent, and compliant tend to be promoted more often than

those considered as average, competent, and compliant. (Knapp)

- Business wardrobe styles change with glacier-like slowness, so there is a high professional risk associated with wearing liberal, faddish styles. (Holton, Holton)
- Most executives would not hire job applicants who presented themselves for a job interview wearing high-fashion clothing. (Molloy)
- Individuals with low self-esteem tend to avoid eye contact. (Knapp)
- Employees avoid eye contact with and seem to dislike superiors who comment un-favorably on the subordinate's performance. (Holton)
- Generally speaking, the less jewelry you wear the more positive impression you make. (Knapp)

A Particularly Noteworthy Finding: Women envision the ideal husband as bearded, masculine, sophisticated and mature. Also, a beard seems to heighten sexual magnetism.

(Freedman)

Don't say things. What you are stands over you the while, and thunders so that I cannot hear what you say to the contrary.

(Ralph Waldo Emerson)

ARE YOU GUILTY OF THE THREE BIGGEST CLOTHES-BUYING MISTAKES?

The three biggest mistakes women make when buying clothes: #1-They let fashion make their decisions; #2-They let their husband, their 'significant other', their best friend or [worst of all] the salesperson make their decisions; #3-They let price make their decision.

Rule of Thumb: When you try on clothing, take a good long look in a full-length mirror. Watch yourself as you bend, sit and move in any way you'll be moving when you wear that clothing. Then look at yourself again. If it docsn't say "WOW!" on you, do not buy it — even if it's the newest fashion, or your shopping partner loves it. The key is — YOU must love it . . and look and feel great in it!

 ## COST PER WEARING FORMULA

This is one of the best ways to assess whether you are putting your money where your time is, in terms of the clothing you wear. As you decide whether a certain article of clothing is worth the cost, use this formula:

$$\frac{\text{COST OF THE ITEM}}{\begin{array}{c}\text{\# OF TIMES}\\\text{YOU WILL WEAR IT}\end{array}}$$

For example, imagine you find a suit jacket that is on sale for $20. It's not a great color for you, and it's a bit tight, but what a bargain! You buy it, wear it once and are so uncomfortable in it you never wear it again! Cost per Wearing=$20.

On the other hand, suppose you saw a wool blend suit on sale for $125. It's your size, a perfect color and style for you, and you could wear it [with a conservative estimate] once a week, for nine months out of the year (36 times/year). The suit will last at least four years (36x4=144 wearings). Cost per wearing = About 86 cents! Now — *that's* a bargain!

LET'S FACE IT

Our face is one of the most expressive parts of our bodies. Researchers suggest that we can make and recognize almost 250,000 distinct facial expressions. Our facial expressions are composed of eight different factors: forehead, brows, lids, eyes, nose, lips, chin and skin.

FOREHEAD: A furrowed brow indicates puzzlement, deep thought, tension, worry, fear, concern. A sweating forehead could mean nervousness or effort. A naturally-wide forehead/receding hairline adds strength of character and maturity. A small forehead or one hidden by hair gives a younger, more casual appearance.

EYEBROWS: Arched brows are dogmatic. Light eyebrows project softness. Penciled-in, thin eyebrows give a more mature, hardened look. Bushy brows project being down to earth. Eyebrows raised to the ceiling show disbelief.

EYELIDS: Sleepy, hooded looks are thought to be cool, slow-moving, in control, detached. Raised, wide-eyed looks mean alertness or interest. An overlong gaze with lids lowered can show sexual interest. Winks can mean warmth, playfulness, sarcasm, kinship.

EYES: The eyes are extremely important in communicating a nonverbal message.

Good eye contact shows interest; comfort with what is being said. Civil inattention (staring) is too dominating and intimidating. A lingering gaze usually connotes sexual interest. Blank stares and shifting/darting eyes usually mean inattention, disinterest. Blinking indicates that a person is absorbing and "processing" information; however, excessive blinking and eye watering shows nervousness, over-emotionalism or weakness.

NOSE: Often we widen our nostrils in fear, rage, extreme nervousness. Rubbing the nose indicates disapproval or resentment. Sometimes we literally "turn up the nose" to show disdain.

LIPS: Full lips make a person look softer, warmer, more sensual. Lips can also part with promise, smirk with certainty, be bitten with nervousness, licked with worry or anticipation. A smile sends the message of rapport, congeniality; a frown shows disapproval. Holding the mouth tight indicates holding back negative or disagreeing thoughts; disgust.

CHIN: Square/angular jawlines are associated with strength; rounded jawlines show warmth and openness. Jutting chins show aggression. Receding chins suggest meekness or lack of character.

SKIN: Blushing shows embarrassment, self-consciousness, weakness, nervousness, lack of confidence. Thin-skinned people appear sensitive, gentle. Thick-skinned people come across as tough, hearty, in control. Firm skin suggests strength, vitality, health. Loose skin projects softness, lack of control.

The face is involved in almost all social interactions. Though there may be other clues, it's usually the principal means by which we recognize each other, judge age and kinship, determine race, or read each other's inner thoughts.

(Shannon Brownlee)

MIRROR IMAGE

Look in the mirror at yourself. Inspect your hair. Toss it (if you have enough). Feel its texture. Note its color and style. Notice your eyes, eyelashes and eyebrows. Reacquaint yourself with their color. Train your eyes on the twin in the mirror. Gaze at the curvature of your eyes. Notice their brightness and intensity; their sadness or happiness. Acknowledge the half-moons under your eyes, if you have them. Check your ears and cheeks. Touch your ears. Pull on them. Examine any blemishes on your face. Lower your gaze to your lips. Notice their size and shape, their color, their tightness or softness. Move your lips. Open your mouth. Inspect your teeth. Assess your chin and neck. Examine any facial hair. Smile at yourself.

Do one thing to improve your looks. Preen yourself. Apply some cosmetics if you wish. Trim your mustache or beard. Brush your teeth. Smile at your double again. Fully engage your eyes again in an extended stare. Appreciate your beauty. Your good looks. Your physical features. Run your fingers over your face a few times. That person is real. That reflection is you. Make it the best you you can!

The best mirror is an old friend.

(George Herbert)

TAKE A LOOK IN THE MIRROR

Dennis Franz, star of NYPD Blue, said: "We all need to look in the mirror and see ourselves as we really are. If we try to make the best of the cards we're dealt, we have a better chance at happiness."

For this is success — to be me . . . and to be the REAL me . . . but to be the best ME that I can be!

TALKATIVENESS

I have found that mature, confident, grounded people monopolize the listening…and that people unsure of themselves monopolize the talking. Talkativeness is an emotional plea for worthiness. It's over-selling the right to speak when the right to speak is a given.

Our self-concept influences how we communicate with others. It determines how we position ourselves during each encounter. It manufactures our reality through perceptual filters, and either frees us to communicate confidently in our surroundings or incarcerates us, causing us to make our nervousness obvious through our incessant chatter.

The cure is difficult...and simple. Difficult because we have to move past our encrusted programming, and simple because all we have to do is remember the advice given by Zeno of Citium: We have been given two ears and but a single mouth, in order that we may listen more and talk less.

SAY WHAT?

For the next two weeks, focus your attention on the skills of asking questions and paraphrasing. Whenever you are talking with a customer or are in meetings, make it *your* responsibility to ask questions and clarify what the other person is saying, or to paraphrase to assure them you have understood. *Remember your goal is to capture the message of the speaker, not to judge, analyze or interpret.* Keep notes of your progress, including your observations of the impact of your efforts.

Focusing on and trusting in the process rather than worrying over the communication outcome has invariably led to the most stimulating and enjoyable conversations in my life.

(Bil Holton)

LISTENING CHECK-UP

Using the Check-Up On Your Listening Quiz on the next page, ask several colleagues, friends, family members and customers to assess your listening skills. This will give you some feedback on how others perceive you as a listener. Use the results to identify one or two specific areas for self-development.

Have them complete the instrument again after you have worked on improving your skills.

	Almost Always	Most of the Time	Rarely
I try to encourage others to participate in the discussion.			
I give good eye contact with the person who is speaking.			
I concentrate on what the other person is saying, rather than preparing what I want to say when it's my turn to talk.			
I let others finish their comments, rather than completing their sentences for them or interrupting with my ideas.			
I ask questions to ensure that I have understood what the other person meant.			
I stay calm and nondefensive when the other person's views differ from mine.			
I show I am listening by using verbal reinforcers (I see; uh huh; yes; go on)			
When taking notes, I focus on writing down key ideas rather than everything that is said.			
I ignore distractions while listening.			
I focus on the message being communicated, without prejudging based on preconceptions or assumptions about the person.			
I avoid distracting nonverbal behaviors during a conversation.			
I spend a greater percentage of the time during the conversation listening than talking.			
TOTAL NUMBER CHECKED:			

To score yourself use the formula on the next page.

A CHECK-UP ON YOUR LISTENING — SCORING

Transfer the Total Number of:

Almost Always: _____ and multiply by 5 = _____
Most of the Time: _____ and multiply by 3 = _____
Rarely: _____ and multiply by 1 = _____

GRAND TOTAL _____

ANALYSIS:

58 - 60   Either you walk on water (keep up the good work), or you lied.

52 - 57   Not bad! You have a lot of good habits, and are using good listening skills to build strong relationships. There are a few areas in which you can improve, so start today!

40 - 51   You're hanging in there about average. You know what to do, but don't always practice it. A little extra effort on your part can bring great rewards, in both your personal and work lives.

28 - 39   Believe it or not, by recognizing your shortcomings you're half-way there! You have many opportunities to improve your listening skills. With increased awareness and practice, you should see benefits immediately!

Below 28 WOW! Perhaps you may not realize what a valuable role listening plays in your success and inner peace. You have considerable challenge ahead to improve your listening — but the payoffs will be tremendous! Select the most critical areas and concentrate on improving them. Take this test again in one month, and reward yourself for your improvement!

The way you stay fresh is you never stop traveling, you never stop listening. You never stop asking people what they think.

(Rene McPherson)

SAY IT WITH STYLE AND PIZZAZZ

Pull together several friends, and have fun doing this activity together. . . or do it all by yourself. Either way, you'll benefit. Select a situation which requires you to communicate "with style." Examples include: handling a customer complaint; telling someone you won't be able to follow through on a commitment; convincing a person to take on a new project; explaining the value of *your* experience, even though it may be less than that of others; asking for a day off; responding to your child's teacher, who claims your child has cheated; confronting your doctor about the long wait you had; handling multiple customers; convincing your spouse to go out for dinner; etc.

Develop two "role plays" to demonstrate your situation. Make one **totally wimpy and ineffective!** Then develop another role play that uses **POWER words and presents a positive impression**. Present your "role plays" *with GUSTO!* It's great if you can do it in front of a mirror, or be videotaped.

It is better to remain silent and be thought a fool than to speak up and remove all doubt!

(Abraham Lincoln)

IT'S ALL IN HOW YOU PERCEIVE IT

Henry Ward Beecher once received in the mail a sheet of paper with one word written on it: Fool. As he held it up, he exclaimed "I've received many messages with no signature, but this is the first time I've received a signature with no message."

START AFFIRMATIVELY

I discovered the following research results in my files; unfortunately I did not record the source of the study. But pay attention to the findings. This study evaluated the initial approach used by 300 individuals who were asking others for something. Of the 300 evaluated, 215 started the conversation with something negative, such as "I hate to bother you . . ."; "Is this a bad time . . ."; or even "Isn't this awful weather we're having?" 85 began positively, with comments such as: "I hope this is a good time to talk . . ."; "I was told you were the person I needed to talk to"; and even "Isn't this great weather?"

Of the 215 who began negatively, only 63 were actually successful in getting what they wanted. Of the 85 who started affirmatively, 78 were successful. While there were undoubtedly other factors involved in the outcome, this is statistically significant!

Take a look at how you begin your requests, and make a commitment to start affirmatively!

ROCKING CHAIR AGREEMENT

A real-estate agent in one of my classes shared that she had a rocking chair in her office, by her desk. She insists that it is very hard for clients to say "NO" when they are rocking back and forth in a YES movement!

THE ART OF REFRAMING

Reframing is a technique whereby you take a comment that is potentially inflammatory, and put it in another perspective that is more positive. This keeps you nondefensive, and puts the conversation on a more positive, solution-focused path.

When Michelle Kwan was being interviewed following the 1998 Winter Olympics, she was asked: "How do you feel about losing the gold?" Michelle came back with what I consider a very mature response: "I didn't lose the gold; I WON the silver!" That's reframing!

FEEDBACK FUNDAMENTALS: WHEN YOU'RE ON THE OFFENSE

One of the toughest types of communication we ever have to do is give constructive criticism to another person. As a result, it is usually done poorly, which only exacerbates the problem. Here are some Feedback Tools to help you provide exceptional and meaningful feedback to others:

- *Keep it private.* No one likes to be criticized in front of others. Bite your tongue and wait until you can be alone with the person.
- *Keep it timely.* Feedback provided too long after the fact is meaningless, and can make a person feel belittled and hopeless. Provide feedback as quickly after the situation occurs as possible.
- *Keep it positively-framed.* Lead into the criticism with a "big-picture" context that helps the individual understand why this is important to them, or demonstrates what they are doing well related to the situation, and why this particular thing is an issue.
- *Keep it specific and descriptive.* Describe actual behavior so the individual can understand what you are talking about. Comments like "You aren't a team player" or "You don't care about my feelings" are too vague and lead to defensiveness rather than behavior changes.
- *Provide examples* of how you'd like to see the behavior changed.
- *Reinforce positive changes.* When the person does

make a change, let them know how much it means to you. People repeat behavior they are rewarded for!

If you are giving this feedback in a work setting, related to performance or work habit issues, schedule a specific follow-up time to assess progress. If the performance has shown no improvement, be bold enough to move ahead with the disciplinary procedure. And don't forget to document!

Constructive criticism is difficult to take — especially *from friends, family members, coworkers, superiors, and strangers.*

A FORMULA FOR FEEDBACK

While I usually dislike a formulamatic approach to communication, it does help sometimes to have a "recipe" to help you frame your feedback to someone about a behavior that bothers you. Here is a formula that works quite well.

"When you . . ." (Describe the behavior)
"I feel . . ." (Describe the effect on you)
"Because . . ." (Describe why the behavior is a
    problem for you)
"In the future, I'd appreciate it if you would . . ."
    (Describe the change you're recommending)

Example: "When you smoke in my car, I feel very irritated because I am allergic to cigarette smoke and have asked you not to smoke around me. In the future, I'd appreciate it if you would put your cigarette out before you get in my car."

STOP "SHOULDING" ON OTHERS

Many communication problems originate from "shoulding" on others! You know what I mean . . . saying things like "You should have told me that"; "You should have included me in that decision"; or "You should have returned that weeks ago." When you "should" on someone, you put them in a no-win situation. They can't change what has already happened, so instead they feel duty-bound to defend their actions.

Instead of "shoulding" on someone, try turning it into a learning experience for them. It's simple! Just replace the phrase "You should have . . ." with the phrase "Next time." Listen to the difference: Instead of "You should have told me that," say "Next time please let me know when you get information like that." Instead of "You should have included me in that decision," say "Next time you have a decision that affects my area, would you include me in the discussion?" This sets the stage for a much more positive interaction, with results that lead to improved communication for everyone.

By the way, try to stop 'shoulding' on yourself so much, too!

P.E.T.'s

Do you talk to yourself? Come on, admit it! Now, a tougher question — do you talk out loud? Even tougher — do you answer? Actually, I believe that those of us who talk to ourselves (I'm proud to admit it!) are truly sane people, because we know good conversationalists when we find them!

Seriously, research claims that we all talk to our-selves, and most of what we say is negative! If you find you're guilty, try using P.E.T.'s. I don't mean house pets, although they do help bring inner peace. What I'm refer-ring to is an acronym. It stands for Personal Empowerment Triggers. P.E.T.'s are short, positive statements that state clearly what you want to achieve or see in your life. They are Personal, because you need to make them specific to your needs; they are Empowering because when you say them, you can actually feel the positive energy flow through your body; and they serve as Triggers to change your behavior and make the state-ment a reality.

Tips for developing effective P.E.T.s:
- *Keep them short.*
- *Keep them positive.* (Say what you want, not what you want to get rid of.) For example, instead of "I am no longer tired," say "I am filled with energy!" In fact, just say both those statements out loud, and feel the difference in your body as you say them.
- *Keep them in the present tense, as if the statements were already true.* Instead of "I will be healthy and fit," say "I am now healthy and fit."
- *Repeat your P.E.T.s often.*

Your word is your wand.
(Florence Scovel Shinn)

It is not enough to know what to say — one must also know how to say it.
(Aristotle)

THE "GAP" ASSESSMENT

Okay, I can hear you now! You're saying "Get real! I know those P.E.T.s aren't true, so what's the point of saying them? I just end up having an internal argument with myself!"

To which I must say, Good point! And you're right. Particularly in the early stages of using P.E.T.s, we get into an emotion versus logic fight in our head. Ignoring our logic is not the answer, because it can be very persistent. I've found that when my logic wants to fight with my P.E.T., I use the GAP Assessment, and fight logic with logic. Here's how it works.

I get out my trusty Self-Development Notebook and use the following formula:

My P.E.T.	My Logic Says:
(write it out)	(write out my logic's argument)

Talk to myself to analyze my Logic's Argument

If My Logic Says:	I Clarify & Specify By:
• All/Every/Never	• Repeating that word as a question (i.e., All? Is that really true?)
• Can't/Must/Should/	• Asking what would really happen if I could? If I did?
• Unspecific (i.e., They...)	• Asking How or Who or What specifically is affecting my desire
• Too... (i.e., I'm too poor; old; fat; dumb)	• Asking "Compared to what?"

Here is an example of what a "GAP Assessment" might look like:

My P.E.T.	My Logic Says:
"I am a very successful sales rep."	"Yeah, right! I never make successful calls. All my cold calls get nipped in the bud. Nobody ever wants to return my calls. I'm just too stupid to do this job."
Talk to myself to analyze my Logic's Argument	
If My Logic Says:	**I Clarify & Specify By:**
• All/Every/Never "I never make successful calls." "All my cold calls get nipped in the bud."	• Repeating that word as a question "Never? Is that true? Is there at least one call I've made that was successful?" "All? Has every call I've made resulted in rejection? Can I think of even one time it was successful?"
• Unspecific (i.e., They...) "Nobody ever wants to return my calls."	• Asking Who specifically is affecting my desire?" "Who specially doesn't return my calls? Do some people return my calls? Who? Why? Can I see a pattern/ What can I learn?"
• Too... (i.e., I'm too poor; old; fat; dumb) "I'm just too stupid to do this job."	• Asking "Compared to what?" "Too stupid compared to who? A seasoned rep who has been doing this for ten years? How can I learn more – improve my skills?"

Once you've spent some time logically analyzing your objections to your P.E.T., it becomes much easier to move through the resistance to action. You begin to identify very specific barriers, and can plan ways to overcome them. For example, in the sample above, one major barrier seems to be a low self image and confidence, perhaps based on a lack of skill in how to conduct effective cold calls. Possible actions that can lead this person to becoming their vision (" . . . a very successful sales rep") could be to take a course in cold calling techniques; work with a sales rep who is very successful at cold calls; track the calls that have been successful to identify what worked; etc.

It is more fun to talk with someone who doesn't use long, difficult words but rather short, easy words like "What about lunch?"

(Pooh's Little Instruction Book)

START YOUR DAY WITH A P.E.T.

There's nothing better than starting your day with a powerful P.E.T., to get you off to a great start! If you notice you tend to wake up with thoughts like "Yuk! Another morning!" try saying instead: "I greet this day with joy and inner peace. I look and feel terrific!"

BLOOD OR ROSES? Florence Atkinson shares an experience of teaching kindergarten in a school for blind children. Five-year-old John (who was sufficiently sighted to recognize color, but not form) was finger-painting with bright red paint. When both his hands were completely covered with the paint, he cupped them, turned to Florence and said: "Look at my hands! They look like they're . . ."

As he paused in the middle of his thought, Florence was anticipating the rest of his sentence to be . . . bloody. Instead he said: ". . . full of red roses!" Florence shared that his imagination made such an impression on her that she often remembers to "Think Beauty" in the midst of unpleasantness, and to always speak from a positive perspective!

 A participant in one of my workshops made this observation: Communicate — it's not just an action verb; it's an action!

SAY IT RIGHT!

These are real classified ads that appeared in news-papers:

Lost: One small apricot poodle. Neutered, like one of the family.

Dinner Special: Turkey $2.35; Chicken or Beef $2.25; Children $2.00

For sale: antique desk suitable for lady with thick legs and large drawers.

Illiterate? Write today for free help.

OOPS . . . . . .

Meanings don't always translate the way we intend. No wonder we have problems in our day-to-day communications. Even corporate Marketing Departments make blunders. Consider these major marketing faux-pas.

When Coca-Cola first entered the Chinese market, the bottles were embossed with the Chinese characters which represented the sounds of "Coca-Cola," but which in fact literally meant "Bite the wax tadpole" or "female horse stuffed with wax," depending on the dialect. In Taiwan, the translation of the Pepsi slogan "Come alive with the Pepsi Generation" came out as "Pepsi will bring your ancestors back from the dead." In Chinese, the Kentucky Fried Chicken slogan "finger-lickin' good" translated to "eat your fingers off."

When General Motors introduced the Chevy Nova in South America, no one could understand why it didn't sell. Then someone realized that "no va" means "it won't go."

FAX IT!

An indication of the difficulty arising from communicating without seeing a person is demonstrated in a cartoon, which shows a man talking on the telephone.

He is saying to the person on the other end of the telephone conversation, "Could you fax me a copy of your facial expression?"

BE CLEAR ABOUT ACRONYMS

This example comes from one of my workshop participants, Jeannie, who is in Customer Service with one of the telephone companies. She said that she was in her doctor's office for a physical, and the nurse was looking at her file. The nurse looked up and said, "Oh, I see you're on PCP."

Jeannie indignantly replied, "No, I'm not! I've never taken drugs in my life!"

The nurse apologized for the misunderstanding and clarified, "No, PCP stands for the Personal Care Plan you have through your company."

DANCE A FEW STEPS IN THEIR SHOES

In our ballroom dancing lessons, our instructors occasionally ask Bil or I to dance each other's part (Bil do the lady's step, or I do the man's). This helps us understand what it feels like, so we can be more responsive to our partner. Try the same thing in communications. Hear your communication from the other person's viewpoint to help you be clearer and more precise in what you say.

THE CHAIR

There's nothing like experience to understand another person's point of view. This was brought home to me vividly in a recent workshop I conducted. It was held at the client's site, and several people rolled their own desk chairs into the meeting room. One of the activities required people to move around and work in different groups. All of a sudden, the Comptroller yelled out,

"Who's chair is this? It is the most uncomfortable thing I've ever sat in!"

His secretary stood up and said, "That's what I've been trying to tell you for months!"

He looked somewhat sheepish, then said, "When we get back to our office, write yourself a requisition for a new chair!"

There's nothing like experience!

FACTS VERSUS PASSION

You've got to do your homework and have the supporting material to prove your points, but at the end of the day, it's passion that wins the decision.

The vacuum created by a failure to communicate will quickly be filled with rumor, misrepresentation, drivel and poison.

(Dennis Waitely)

NAMES MEAN A LOT

Use an individual's name when you talk with them. It builds rapport, increases the willingness to cooperate, and enhances the relationship.

WHAT SHOULD I CALL YOU?

Two examples flash into my mind instantly when the topic of people's names comes up. The first goes back to my distant past, in my first marriage. Being very young and a little intimidated by my husband's parents, I was unsure exactly what to call them. I never clarified it — never asked — just found ways to avoid calling them by any name. It became a most distressing and frustrating issue for me, and the longer it went on, the more difficult it was to bring up. The matter was resolved when the marriage ended in divorce. But I never forgot how terrible it felt, and how idiotic I was to never resolve it. When I met my current husband's parents for the first time, I asked, "What would you like me to call you?" We clarified it up front, and it was never an issue!

The second experience comes from one of my workshops. I was conducting a five-series session with a group of Systems Engineers. A new person was hired, and joined our training program at the third session. Her name was Lucia, and I asked her how to pronounce it. She said "Loo-chee´-a. Thank you so much for asking. It gets pronounced like Loos´-ee-a all the time." I wrote her name phonetically in my notes, so I'd remember. During that session, we happened to be talking about using our customer's name, and I used Lucia as an example. One of the other participants said, "Thank you for that example!" Then he looked directly at Lucia and said, "Lucia, I haven't used your name at all because I was embarrassed that I couldn't remember how to pronounce it. So I just avoided it . . . and you. Now I can call you by the right name!" Lucia gave a huge smile, and said, "Now I know why you've avoided me. I thought you just didn't like me."

ROLE INTEGRITY

I find that the more flexible and non-judgmental I am when I meet people, the more pleasant my interactions are. I rely on my inner director to choose the appropriate role for me. For instance, I am aware that changing my communication style depending on the circumstance — discussing the intricacies of formulating mission, vision, and values with a client; giving one of my sons parental advice; listening to my ballroom dance instructor comment on my last pivot and sway; asking my husband for his wise counsel — do not make me an inconsistent person. All of these behaviors are a part of my communication competence. I am free to choose the role I should play in any given situation, and I trust that my inner guide knows how I should react so that my communication objectives are met.

To be nobody but yourself in a world which is doing its *best, night and day, to make you everybody else — means to fight the hardest battle which any human being can fight and never stop fighting.*

(e.e. cummings)

WHITE MEAT OR DARK?

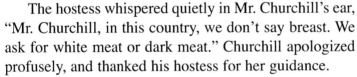

The story is told of a visit to America by Winston Churchill, during which he attended a buffet luncheon where cold fried chicken was served. Returning for a second helping, he asked the server, "May I have some breast, please?"

The hostess whispered quietly in Mr. Churchill's ear, "Mr. Churchill, in this country, we don't say breast. We ask for white meat or dark meat." Churchill apologized profusely, and thanked his hostess for her guidance.

The following morning, the lady received a beautiful orchid from Mr. Churchill, with an accompanying card that read: "I would be most obliged if you would pin this on your white meat."

VERBAL PLACEBOS

Meeting Professional International Board Member: You really believe in affirmations, don't you?

Cher: Positive affirmations are prescriptions for health. If repeated often enough…and enthusiastically enough, I believe they can be powerful placebos.

MPI Board Member: Placebos? You mean they're fake?

Cher: Placebo effects *are* real. The medical profession has used placebos consistently and with great success for years. As verbal placebos, affirmations imprint positive thoughts into our subconscious, causing it to endorse what is claimed at face value. Our subconscious believes these repeated messages and magnetizes experiences to manifest what we are claiming.

MPI Board Member: You mean, if I say: *I am a rich, well and happy meeting planner* — I'll be one?

Cher: If you'll conscientiously repeat that affirmation enough times, believing it's already true on some level, you'll be able to neutralize old, negative inner scripts and build new, more positive ones. This switch in consciousness from doubt to possibility is an empowering process. This is a long answer to your short question; but, yes, I believe if you believe you can, you can. And I believe affirmations can accelerate your progress to meet meaningful goals. Of course, you also have to 'move your feet!'

BUT WHAT ABOUT AND?

Whenever you use the word "but," the person you are talking with perceives that you disagree with them. It also discounts anything positive you have already said. For example, if you say "I think your new hairstyle is beautiful, but it's really short," the person automatically assumes you hate it because it's too short. If instead you say, "I think your new hairstyle is beautiful — and it's really short!," the person feels you gave them a compliment! Try replacing your "but" with "and" for improved communications.

LOOK FOR WAYS TO PRAISE

Consider the results of a study reported in "Selling is a Woman's Game": A psychology professor sent out cards to a dozen acquaintances, selected randomly, with the same message: "Congratulations! You should be very proud."

Everyone who received a card replied with hearty thanks, reporting new promotions, grandchildren, a new home, or a personal victory of some sort. Many were surprised by the professor's acknowledgment, but all felt they had something to be praised about.

PEOPLE THRIVE ON PRAISE

What does the research summarized above say to us? People thrive on praise, and most people do have things happening in their lives that deserve praise. It's relatively easy to find something positive to say to people, if we just keep our eyes open. My personal philosophy: There are two types of people who respond well to praise: men and women!

Good communication is as stimulating as black coffee, and just as hard to sleep after."

(Anne Morrow Lindbergh)

ACCEPT COMPLIMENTS: Gene Godwin, one of my clients, observed that we believe anything another person says about us as long as it's derogatory, but for some reason we have trouble believing and accepting a compliment!

❝ ❗ ❞ *If people around you will not hear you, fall down before them and beg their forgiveness, for in truth you are to blame.*

(Fyodor Dostoyevsky)

❝ ❗ ❞ *If I ignore the emotional plea and respond only to the words, I will not be communicating with you, there will not be a flow of understanding between us.*

(Hugh Prather)

BUILDING A PROSPERITY CONSCIOUSNESS

BUILDING A PROSPERITY
CONSCIOUSNESS — *SNEAK PEEK*

One of the biggest challenges most people face in terms of experiencing inner peace is financial. I cannot tell you how many times I hear the words: "If I only had the money. . ." Nothing can upset your emotional apple-cart more than a sense of financial lack. Perhaps the greatest gift we can give to ourselves is the gift of a prosperity consciousness, because it transcends the issue of money. It moves us into a deeper recognition of prosperity as an attitude about life rather than a condition we find ourselves in.

Let's start by understanding what PROSPERITY really means, as I use the term in this chapter. Webster has three words that relate to this concept: PROSPER — to succeed, thrive and grow vigorously; PROSPERITY — prosperous condition; good fortune, wealth, success; PROSPEROUS — 1. prospering; flourishing; 2. well-to-do; well-off; 3. conducive to success; favorable.

Notice the word vigorously in Webster's definition. That implies more that just succeeding. It indicates a flow — a rush — a powerful movement toward a result. Prosperity is not static — it is not something that just sort of trickles into your life. It is dynamic — it is exciting — and it requires active initiative to get results.

Let's go to some other "experts" to get a clearer look at what prosperity means. Catherine Ponder, in her book *Dynamic Laws of Prosperity*, defines prosperity as "having peace, health and plenty in all areas of your life." Jack Addington's definition, in *All About Prosperity* and *How You Can Prosper*, says "prosperity is the ability to achieve; to be what you want to be; to do what you would like to do; the ability to express your God-given talents; the ability to draw upon the infinite resources of God right where you are and make them a part of your own experience." Another writer, Margaret Stevens, claims that prosperity is "the ability to do what you want to do when you want to do it." She emphasizes that many people are materially wealthy, but are in great poverty when it comes to friendship and inner peace of mind. Others have everything but money.

There is much more to prosperity than simply having money. And yet, we can't overlook the fact that money is one piece of the puzzle. We live in a society that is very materialistic, while at the same time instilling guilt trips on you if you have too much of something. The psychology of prosperity is very interesting, for — believe it or not — it has nothing to do with the amount of money you make or the amount of possessions you have. It has everything to do with your consciousness — your inner awareness of how you feel about where you are at this moment, and what ability you have to respond to your needs as they arise. And so, we cannot overlook the role money plays in our peace of mind. The trick is to use your money without letting your money control you, and to develop a consciousness that internalizes the principles of prosperity in your daily living.

A perfect analogy is the thermometer versus the thermostat. Think about your living room. What does the thermometer on the wall do? Of course — it records the temperature in the room. If the room gets cooler, the thermometer goes down. If it gets warmer in the room, the thermometer reading goes up. It simply reacts to the environment. On the other hand, think about your thermostat. What does it do? Right — it controls the environment in the room. You set it to create the temperature you desire. Which are you like — the thermometer or the thermostat? Do you simply react to situations around you? Do you sit around wishing you would win the lottery — or pray an unknown rich relative would die and leave you the family fortune? Do you blame your boss or your family or your friends or an illness for your financial problems? OR — are you more like a thermostat? Do you actively control your environment? Do you go after the goals you desire, and meet obstacles with a positive, success-oriented attitude? Do you positively apply the prosperity principles to create a more fulfilling, exciting and prosperous life?

In this powerful chapter, you will discover the principles of a prosperity consciousness, and learn how to put them into practice in your everyday life. By applying the principles and tools from this section, you will experience a quantum leap in your ability to handle the frustrations of apparent lack and, regardless of the outer appearances, you will see phenomenal growth in your sense of inner peace.

GIVE GLADLY

It is so easy to get depressed when you are writing checks to pay bills. The focus tends to hover on that diminishing bottom line with each subtraction, and our recognition of our lack takes front and center stage.

Make a mental shift into prosperity consciousness with this simple technique. On each check, as you fill it out, write the word "Gladly" above the words "Pay to the Order of..." This acknowledges your appreciation that this creditor trusted you enough to give you something without demanding immediate payment. It also reinforces your joy in having the money available to pay what is owed.

PEOPLE NOTICE

I routinely write "Gladly" on every check I write, 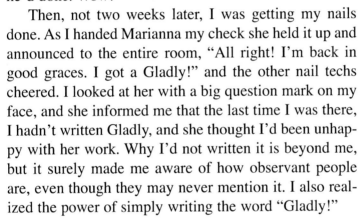 and wondered if anyone else ever noticed. Then I got a "double whammy" from the universe. When I went to get my hair done, Richard, my hairdresser, commented on how neat it was that I always wrote gladly on my checks. He said it made him feel good about the work he'd done. Wow!

Then, not two weeks later, I was getting my nails done. As I handed Marianna my check she held it up and announced to the entire room, "All right! I'm back in good graces. I got a Gladly!" and the other nail techs cheered. I looked at her with a big question mark on my face, and she informed me that the last time I was there, I hadn't written Gladly, and she thought I'd been unhappy with her work. Why I'd not written it is beyond me, but it surely made me aware of how observant people are, even though they may never mention it. I also realized the power of simply writing the word "Gladly!"

One of my friends made this haunting observation.  She said, "I find it so much easier to give when I don't have much. When I get a windfall in my checking account, I suddenly turn into a miser, protecting it, fearing I'll lose it. But when I'm operating on my usual paycheck to paycheck mentality, I am generous almost to a fault!"

PAY TAXES GLADLY?

My biggest personal challenge in writing "Gladly" is  for checks I write to the Government for taxes related to our business. For the longest time, I just couldn't bring myself to do it. It felt too phony, since in actuality, I resented the amount the government demanded.

Then our Mastermind Partner came up with an idea that's helped. He suggested that I choose a few government-funded programs I really support and then imagine my checks are donations to those programs. Now I'm able to write Gladly — and I have a much better attitude about writing those checks.

SIMPLE INDULGENCE

Look for little things that give you the feeling of prosperity. It's amazing how simple it can be. For me, it's always having an unopened box of laundry detergent and dishwasher powder available. It lets me be assured I'll never run out at an inopportune time. Another one for me is buying flavored coffee beans, and grinding my own for each cup. The simple pleasure of smelling the freshly-ground beans makes me feel downright extravagant! I also like having a stock of toilet paper in the bathroom closet . . . and candles around my bathtub. Discover your simple indulgences to give yourself a feeling of richness, which strengthens your prosperity consciousness and your self image as well.

 I'd rather have roses on my table than diamonds on my neck.

(Emma Goldman)

SAVE A LITTLE, MISS A LOT

I stood in a bookstore recently and watched a well-dressed couple discuss the utility of purchasing an important financial book. He thumbed through the pages, pointed out a few kernels of financial wisdom which leaped out at them from its pages, and told her how impressed he was at both the writing and the content. I bit my lip when I saw him turn the book over to see the price and then set it back on the shelf.

"Aren't you going to buy that?" I imposed as I walked up to them.

He said he was going to wait until the book came out in paperback. She nodded her innocent agreement and told me they would either purchase the paperback version or wait until the book was in the library.

I was struck by the fact that this good-looking, intelligent couple, in order to save a *few* dollars, was potentially saying no to *hundreds* of dollars. Any one of the ideas in that book could help them achieve wealth *sooner* than *later*. How often do we make decisions that save a little, and sacrifice a lot?

If money is your hope for independence, you will never have it. The only real security… in this world is a reserve of knowledge, experience and ability.

(Henry Ford)

PROSPERITY AFFIRMATION

Whenever you find yourself becoming overwhelmed by financial difficulties, make a conscious choice to reframe your thinking. Affirm, out loud if possible, the following truth: "I am prosperous. Everything I need now comes to me, in accordance with Divine Order. I live in a universe of prosperity, and my prosperity comes to me in many ways. I expect the unexpected, and give thanks."

CAPTURING THE ESSENCE

Identify something you really want, and have not been able to afford. Write that item at the top of a sheet of paper. Under it, make a list of as many things as possible that describe the *essence* of what you want. In other words, what will having this item bring you? Here's an example:

A New Home
- Openness
- Clean and fresh
- Quiet place (meditation room)
- Good place to entertain
- New appliances
- Bright colors
- Larger Bedroom — more space, etc.

Review the list of "essences" and ask yourself: *What can I do right now, with what I have, to bring me some of this essence?* For the example above, perhaps you can cordon off a meditation area in the corner of a room; bring in small bunches of fresh flowers; paint a wall a bright primary color; do some form of creative entertaining in the space you have.

Sometimes, by capturing the essence of what we want, we fulfill our need completely. It also helps us to be more patient in the waiting, and more specific in our visualizations.

> My personal definition for prosperity is this: I am prosperous when I never have to do something I don't want to do, just because of money, and when I never don't do something I want to do, just because of money.

THE LAW OF ATTRACTION

If you take a good look around, you will notice that there really is no lack of money — just a problem with distribution! The good news is, we have the ability to attract some of that money our way. Just apply the timeless Law of Attraction: We draw into our experience that which we believe and accept for ourselves. What we focus on is what we attract.

The Law of Attraction, like all principles, is true, regardless of whether you believe it or not. It works, whether you focus on positive or negative. So let's put it to work in a positive way! Take a look at what you focus on; your thoughts are like a magnet, attracting experiences to you like metal shavings!

Make an effort to concentrate on the positive side of everything you experience. By picturing the best for yourself and for others, you put the dynamic Law of Attraction to work in a positive way in your life.

PUTTING THE LAW OF ATTRACTION TO WORK

Here is a list of seven specific actions you can take immediately, to begin using the Law of Attraction to bring greater prosperity into your life. I recommend that you label one section of your Self-Development Journal as "Prosperity Attraction," and keep track of what you do and the results you experience.

- Whenever you spend your money, take a moment to bless it as it goes out, and claim a ten-fold return on it.
- Keep a record of exactly how you are spending your money. Write down every expenditure, non-judgmentally, and at the end of each week evaluate your spending habits. Sometimes we spend money without realizing where it goes, and end up using our resources for unimportant things. This shortchanges us when there is something we really want to do. (You might find that you can buy tickets to see that theatre production if you are willing to pack your lunch instead of eating at the deli every day.)

- Observe the spending habits of people who have more money than you do. Talk with them if you can, and simply ask them for the best advice they can give on how to have more financial resources available. Watch how they make decisions, and how they use the money they have.
- Use Prosperity Affirmations on a regular basis. Write your own one-sentence statements, such as: "I have all the money I need to pay my bills, with plenty to share and spare."; or "Money flows to me."; or "God is my source, and I attract all the money I desire."
- Evaluate your attitudes about money. We are often our own worst enemy when it comes to a Prosperity Consciousness. Catch yourself whenever you are thinking poverty thoughts, such as "I can't afford this," "Money is the root of all evil," or "It's not right to have too much money."
- Respect money and treat it well. Keep it neatly in your billfold. Acknowledge its value as an exchange for goods and services. Recognize the good that it can bring when you spend it wisely. Focus on ways you can give money for positive purposes.
- Make a list of what you would do if you had a large sum of money. Be very specific. It is amazing how money finds its way to you when you have specific uses for it. So make your plans, and determine how much money you would need to make those dreams a reality.

The strongest single factor in prosperity consciousness is self-esteem: believing you can do it, believing you deserve it, believing you will get it.

(Jerry Gillies)

MONEY STAYS WHERE IT'S WELL-TREATED

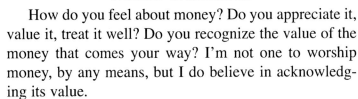

How do you feel about money? Do you appreciate it, value it, treat it well? Do you recognize the value of the money that comes your way? I'm not one to worship money, by any means, but I do believe in acknowledging its value.

When you receive money in any form (from a penny you find on the street to your pay check or a surprise gift), take a moment to bless it, to be thankful that the money has come into your life. Affirm that it will multiply as you use it for good. Remember, money goes where it's invited, and stays where it's well-treated!

An Editorial Comment in the Raleigh News & Observer: "You reported that the legislature considered a bill restricting fortune telling and predicting the future for money . . . If (fortune tellers) would increase their fees and relabel themselves consultants, there would be no problem."

SELF-MADE?

Eric Butterworth shared a story about a man who brought his boss home for dinner one evening. The boss was a gruff and self-centered man, who talked only about himself and criticized everyone and everything. The man's young son stared at his father's boss all evening. Finally, the boss could stand it no longer. He looked at the little boy and growled: "What are you looking at?" The little boy replied, "My daddy says you are a self-made man." The boss puffed up and egotistically claimed, "That's absolutely right, young man." The little boy looked at him and quietly asked, "But why did you make yourself like that?"

We truly make ourselves what we are. As you look at yourself, do you like what you see? True inner peace comes from within, not without. It is more than money and possessions; it is a feeling of confidence and joy, a focus on others, a recognition of the good that we can give, no matter who we are or how much we have. If you don't like what you see, you have the power to change it. We truly are all self-made.

When we hate something, we become its slave.

DRAW YOUR FINANCIAL BOX — AND THE ESCAPE HATCH

Get a large piece of construction paper, and a box of crayons or magic markers. Take a few minutes, and reflect on the financial situation you are struggling with. In your mind, develop a picture of the issues confronting you, the amount of money you need, the items you wish to purchase, the joys you want to experience.

Once you have a vivid picture of your financial situation in your mind, begin to draw a Financial Problems Box. Make it as large or small as your intuition dictates. Design it with illustrations of your barriers, your needs, and the feelings you have about being financially boxed in.

Now, using a color or colors you haven't used yet, let your intuition help you draw escape hatches in the box. Don't give a lot of thought to this; just let your hand begin to draw. Feel free to use word labels as you draw.

When you are finished with your masterpiece, reflect on what it is saying to you. Very often, ideas will appear that can move you out of the boxed-in feeling toward a resolution to your financial problems.

SEE A PENNY, PICK IT UP . . .

There are those who say that if you see a penny lying on the ground, you should only pick it up if it's showing heads. They claim it's bad luck to pick up a penny that is showing tails.

I believe that any unexpected wealth is welcome. We create our own luck, so I take a conscious action and turn the penny over, so heads is showing. Then I pick it up, bless it, and smile!

I've never seen a Brinks truck follow a hearse to the cemetery.

(Barbara Hutton)

TRUE WEALTH

Small Business Owner: I have all of the things I need, so why don't I feel wealthy?

Cher: Money and objects...material possessions, in general, will not automatically fill your real needs or give you the personal satisfaction you want. Ask yourself what you think having more money and things will do for you. Will you feel more secure? Alive? At peace? More successful? Less inhibited? The envy of your friends and neighbors? More powerful?

View money and things not as something to help you fill a void in your life, but as emotional tools to help you express the real you. Things will never keep you happy for long. You will feel wealthy when what you have represents what you are, not what you think others want you to be.

Never confuse your net worth with your self worth!

MAKING THE MOST OF A SITUATION

I once heard the story of a man who had bought a horse; however, when it was delivered the horse was dead. What to do? The man decided to hold a raffle for the horse. Based on his advertising, he had many participants, and made more than his money back.

When asked if people didn't complain when they discovered the horse was dead, the man explained that the only person who complained was the winner, and he gave him his money back!

Intuition is your guide here. One level of you knows everything there is to know. Find that level, ask for guidance, and trust you'll be led wherever you most need to go.

(Richard Bach)

AT A SURVIVAL LEVEL

MBA Candidate: I don't like living from paycheck to paycheck. Sometimes I wonder if going back to school has been worth it.

Cher: Living at a survival level is no fun, but your schooling is important. You are creating a net worth of skills, education and experience that can be converted into more money when you graduate. Your earning potential is increasing every day you're in school…and you're learning important lessons.

MBA Candidate: Lessons? What kind of lessons?

Cher: Some of the most important kind — Life lessons. For example, you're learning how little it takes to live on. You're learning humility. You're making decisions on what is important to you. You're learning how to trust in faith…How to feel settled and secure without a lot of money. You're also learning how to be generous even though you have but little.

You're learning about cash flow, return on equity, profit and loss.

Part of the experience of working full-time and going to school is postponing things you can do without. Separating the relevant from the trivial is a life enriching skill. Be patient with yourself.

MONEY FACTS

> Paper money was first issued in China in 2697 BC., but did not enter into wide-spread use until the mid 1700's. The first coins, probably bean-shaped gold and silver ingots, were issued by Lydia in the seventh century, BC.

We were so poor when I was a boy...if my mother threw the dog a bone, and the bone had any meat on it, the dog would call for a fair catch.

(Lee Trevino)

DO YOU REALLY WANT IT ALL?

Let me challenge you — even if you *could* "have it all," would you really want it? I spoke recently with one of my clients who shared an interesting piece of information. It seems that three of their employees (from different locations) had all been fairly big winners in their respective state lotteries. I found this a bit unusual, but she assured me it was true. I then inquired about how the different employees had responded to the good fortune. She grimly commented that they had all left the company; but they'd only heard from one of them — the other two had not even bothered to call and resign formally. They just never showed up again! The one who did respond shared a pitiful story of how people suddenly flocked to her home, with stories of need and demands for assistance. One family actually brought their daughter, in a wheelchair, and for two months parked her outside their home with a big sign, stating that the girl needed X amount of dollars for corrective surgery. This big winner said more times than my client could count that she wished she had never won the money. It just wasn't worth it!

Now, this doesn't mean that money is bad. In fact, when I share this story with audiences, most of the people say, "Just give me that chance! I can deal with the problems!" But I urge you to really consider what is most important to you . . . and set your goals in that area.

> Prosperity is experiencing balance in life; it is attaining what we want on mental, physical, emotional, spiritual, and financial levels…(It) is the natural result of opening our minds to our creative imaginations and being willing to act on our ideas.   (Ruth Ross)

The spendthrift cannot succeed, mainly because he stands eternally in fear of poverty.

(Napoleon Hill)

THIS OR SOMETHING BETTER

When Life Experience kicks you in the teeth — challenging your entire belief system about prosperity consciousness — learn to say 'thank you', and affirm 'this, or something better.' I remember when we lived in a condominium, and were desperately trying to sell it so we could move into a house. It had been on the market for almost a year, and we finally got a buyer. We were ecstatic, and immediately began our search for a house. We found one quickly, and made a contingency offer on it, based on closing the sale of our home, never doubting it would happen.

Imagine our disappointment when our agent contacted us and told us the sale had fallen through. We were devastated. But we really do work on applying these principles, and we looked at each other and said, "Okay. It must be 'something better.' Let's celebrate this falling through."

I must admit it was a little forced, but the point is, we did it! And I am pleased to report that about six months later we had a marvelous experience working with a builder in designing the home we now live in. It is infinitely better than the one we'd originally wanted, and it serves as a constant reminder to us to trust God that if we don't get what we think we want, something better is in store!

GUILT TRIP

It's time to grab a notebook and pen again, and jot down any thoughts you have in response to the following question: What feelings of guilt do I have related to being rich?

Give yourself time to really think about this one. It may be that you feel guilty because a friend of yours is going through financial difficulties while you're not; perhaps you have a belief that rich is not spiritual; maybe you feel you didn't 'suffer' enough to earn your money; maybe you're having too much fun while others are struggling at their jobs. Assess your own Guilt Trips, and plan a new route to travel.

LIQUID MONEY

High School Graduate: What can I do to start feeling financially secure? I don't have a whole lot of money, so take it easy on what you recommend.

Cher: Save your change everyday. Put it in some kind of container and when you've filled it, deposit all of it in a money market fund.

High School Graduate: Just my pocket change?

C   h   e   r   :

You can add dollar bills, but the idea is to program yourself to save small amounts of money. You'll be surprised at how quickly your change adds up. Do not dip into your *pot of gold*. You must discipline yourself to leave the change in the bank. Now, that's a start. I repeat, the pocket change idea is only a start. Financial security is a state of mind...and a disciplined practice of investing money wisely.

High School Graduate: What can I do next...to feel like I'm making headway?

Cher: Maintain a liquid money fund. It's an emergency insurance fund. Use your pocket change stash to build a savings account equal to three or four months' worth of the total bills you owe each month. The money should be as liquid as possible and earn the highest interest rate possible. This emergency fund won't produce wealth, but it'll certainly protect you from an unexpected crisis. Deposit at least 10% of any financial windfall into the account. Re-supply the emergency account whenever you have to dip into it. Be disciplined, and you'll be amazed at how quickly your change changes your feelings about prosperity!

We took our first overseas vacation from money we had saved by collecting our change at the end of each day. I was overwhelmed at how quickly it added up. It made me realize how little amounts of money can multiply and grow. It also made me realize that we are richer than we know. For some reason, we only see the value in large sums of money, in big bills. But the little coins add up to create those big sums.

THE MULTIPLYING POWER OF MONEY

It is really amazing how quickly money can multiply. Imagine you are offered a job for one month. You have the choice of earning $100 a day, or starting out at a penny for the first day, with your salary doubling each day. Which would you take?

Believe it or not, you should start out at a penny. At the end of 30 days, you will earn $5,368,709.12 — just for day 30! If you choose the $100 a day, at the end of thirty days, you will have earned a *total* of $3,000.00.

The moral: Prosperity can begin in small ways, and multiply exponentially! Don't keep waiting for that huge windfall — that big lottery win — the prize winning number in the Publisher's Clearing House Sweepstakes. Focus on the little sources of prosperity, and let them multiply in your life.

Broke is a temporary condition. Poor is a state of mind.
(Hollis Norton)

WHAT IS A POVERTY CONSCIOUSNESS?

A poverty consciousness is mostly an expressed sense of lack, a lowered sense of self-worth, a feeling of inadequacy when it comes to managing money. People who struggle with finances generally believe one or more of the following. They:

- believe you've got to get yours while the getting is good;
- have a fear of losing what they have;
- think there's virtue in poverty;
- *expect* to run out of money before they run out of calendar each month;
- accept poverty as their station in life;
- refuse to invest what little money they have;
- believe it's okay to get something for nothing;
- always look for the cheapest way to do anything (even at the expense of time, energy or self-esteem)
- quibble over cents
- fail to invest in themselves.

Do a check-up on your own beliefs, and if you identify even one of the above as active in your life, take steps to reprogram your thoughts and actions toward a more "Prosperity-Consciousness" approach.

Whenever you feel a heaviness, a resistance, or a reluctance to continue, it is a sign that you are not following your highest path.

(Sanaya Roman and Duane Packer)

THE LAW OF GIVING AND RECEIVING

Life is based on the principle of giving and receiving: if you are not receiving the good you want and feel you deserve, take a look at what you are giving. When you give, it comes back to you multiplied! This is, perhaps, the most exciting prosperity principle I know.

The Bible supports this principle: "Give, and it shall be given to you; good measure, pressed down, shaken together, running over, will they put into your lap. For the measure you give will be the measure you get back" (Luke 6:38).

John Bunyan said: "There was a man, they called him mad; The more he gave, the more he had." Begin to search for ways you can give to others, for their enrichment, fulfillment and enjoyment. According to this guiding principle, you will experience abundance in your life as a result.

Some luck lies in not getting what you thought you wanted but getting what you have, which once you have got it you may be smart enough to see is what you would have wanted had you known.

(Garrison Keillor)

LEARN HOW TO RECEIVE

I never cease to be amazed at how difficult it is to be a good receiver. I'm not talking about a football player (although I imagine it's a pretty tough role, too). I'm talking about being on the receiving end of a gift from another person — even something as simple as a compliment. Ever notice how we respond? Someone says, "What a great outfit that is!" We respond, "Oh, this old thing? I've had it for years." Or someone says: "Congratulations on that great presentation you gave."

Our response? "I thought I really messed up, especially during the QandA."

I recently heard a woman who was complimented on a beautiful suit she was wearing go into a ten minute dissertation on how cheap it was, where she had purchased it, and how it didn't fit quite right! More than the compliment-giver wanted to hear, I'm sure!

The Law of Giving and Receiving requires us to be good at receiving as well as giving. There is a very simple technique to apply. Whenever anyone gives you anything (a compliment, money, a gift), look them in the eye, smile and sincerely say, "Thank you."

HOW TO HANDLE DEBT

Worrying about your debts is a waste of time. Wishing they didn't exist is useless. Instead, use your energy to learn from, and recover from, the situation. Here are a few things to do immediately:

- Contact each debtor and arrange for a way to pay a portion of what you owe. Creditors will usually be thrilled that someone is willing to deal with the situation.
- Forgive yourself for anything you have done to create the situation.
- Write a "pretend check" to pay off the debts. Visualize each statement being sent to you with the words PAID IN FULL written across it.
- Analyze your financial situation, and ask yourself what lesson(s) you can learn from the experience to apply in the future. For example, you might be learning a lesson about: trust; being able to ask for help; getting by on less than you thought possible; finding prosperity in things other than money; how to give even when you have no money.

• Reframe your thinking and your words to reflect a prosperity consciousness. Rather than saying "I can't afford that," say "I choose not to buy that right now." When someone asks you how things are going, don't give in to the temptation of complaining about your money woes. Instead, report on the good things that are happening in your life. Focus on something positive.

I bargained with life for a penny
And Life would give no more,
However I begged at evening
As I counted my scanty store.
For life is a just employer —
It pays you what you ask.
But once you have set the wages
Then you must bear the task.
I worked for a menial's hire
Only to learn — dismayed —
*That **any** wage I would have asked of Life*
Life would have willingly paid.

(Anonymous)

THE PROSPERITY DOZEN

Make a list of a dozen things that you enjoy doing, and you will never be bored.

Make a list of a dozen ways you can earn money, and you will never have to worry about being broke.

Make a list of a dozen skills, talents and abilities you have, and you will never have to worry about losing a job, or be intimidated by life's setbacks or the criticism of others.

THE LAW OF VACUUM

Get rid of what you don't want to make room for what you do want! This is the Prosperity Principle of Vacuum. Whenever you are willing to take a risk and create a vacuum, it will be filled. This is not just some vague, philosophical mumbo-jumbo. It is a real, practical principle. I challenge you to test it out. Here are two examples of how it has worked for others:

1. One of my clients called me excitedly to report that he had tried the Law of Vacuum in his business. He took a risk by releasing the customers who were not giving him the return on his investment of time and energy. He transferred their accounts to younger salespeople who really appreciated his generosity. He admitted he was a little scared, for by giving the accounts away, he left a void in his income that was pretty dramatic. However, he began to market to a different type of clientele in creative ways, and almost instantly, he attracted new clients — larger accounts which provided a much better return on his investment of time and energy.

2. A friend of mine was despondent about her professional wardrobe. She had recently been promoted, but did not have the resources to purchase the kind of clothing she needed to wear in her new position. She shared how she tried out the Law of Vacuum by going through her closet and getting rid of anything she no longer needed. She said she felt a twinge of panic as she looked at her near empty closet! The very next day, her cousin dropped by with a huge box of clothes, saying, "I cleaned out my closet and had these suits I can't fit in anymore. I think they may fit you." Suddenly my friend had a wardrobe of several beautiful suits that fit her like they were tailor-made.

The basic secret of unlimited prosperity is this: God is the Source of (our) supply, and He has provided many channels through which the riches of the universe can flow to (us).
(Catherine Ponder)

CHECK OUT YOUR MONKEY TRAPS

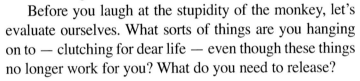

Do you know how they capture monkeys in southeast Asia? It's very interesting. They design a container about the size of a shoe box. On one end they drill a hole, just large enough for the monkey's hand to fit in. Then they fill the box with fruit and lock it. The monkey smells the fruit and sticks his hand in the box. But once he's wrapped his hand around the fruit, his fist is too big to fit back through the hole. He jumps up and down, screaming, but even as he sees the hunters approach, he will **not** let go of the fruit to free himself.

Before you laugh at the stupidity of the monkey, let's evaluate ourselves. What sorts of things are you hanging on to — clutching for dear life — even though these things no longer work for you? What do you need to release?

BUY IT

Think of a small sum of money that you could afford to spend right now that wouldn't rock your financial apple cart. Just for fun think of ten things you could spend the *extra* money on, things that would bring you happiness and joy.

Pick one of those things that would represent a meaningful purchase, and buy it! Splurge a little, realizing you won't do this often. Enjoy the purchase. Consider buying another item from your list of ten. Budget for it. Reward yourself for your money management.

What is important is having enough money to do the work you came to do, and not having so much that it keeps you from the work you came to do.

(Sanaya Roman)

FINANCIAL HEALTH CHECK-UP

My accountant, Jim Woodruff, CPA, gave this sound advice in a newsletter he sent to his clients. See what it says to you.

There is no time better than now to review your overall financial health. A self diagnosis will help you determine any areas of weakness or uncertainty.

Personal Finance — Living within Your Means. Do you have a monthly budget? Do you know where your money is going? Is your consumer debt under control or does it control you?

Insurance — Planning for Disasters. Do you have adequate life and disability insurance to maintain your current lifestyle? Are you protecting your assets with sufficient homeowner's and personal liability insurance? Is your health insurance sufficient?

Investments — Making Your Money Work for You. Are your assets properly invested? Is the rate of return sufficient for the degree of risk you are taking? Are you comfortable with the risk level? Are your investments diversified?

Retirement — Planning for the Golden Years. Do you have an established savings plan for retirement funded with pre-tax dollars that will grow tax-free? Is this retirement savings adequate to maintain your current lifestyle at your retirement age? Have you planned for health care costs through long-term care insurance?

Savings — Achieving Your Dreams. Do you have a plan to fund your children's education? Are you saving for special family goals such as a new home?

Estate — Planning for Those You Leave Behind. Do you have a will? Does it say who will be the guardian of your minor children? Will you owe significant estate taxes (rates are higher than income tax rates)? Have you done planning to minimize your estate taxes? Do you have a Durable Power of Attorney and a Medical Power of Attorney? Have you planned for the ownership and management succession of any family-owned business?

Facts do not cease to exist because they are ignored.
(William S. Burroughs)

DOLLARS AND SENSE

Refrain from spending money you don't have for things you don't need to impress friends you don't like or relatives you seldom see. Someone once said that dollars and sense should go together. The more dollars you have, the more uncommon sense you'll need.

By all means enjoy the fruits of your labor. Your money is … your money! Spend it like you want to spend it, but spend it wisely. Managing your wealth wisely can bring you many opportunities. Mismanaging it can leave you bankrupt — financially, emotionally and spiritually.

It's your money. You earned it. Consider holding on to some of it. Invest a portion of it now. We're only talking dollars and sense.

Whatever you have — spend less.
(Samuel Johnson)

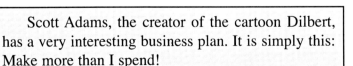

Scott Adams, the creator of the cartoon Dilbert, has a very interesting business plan. It is simply this: Make more than I spend!

Practice self-denial and self-control, as well as the strictest economy in all financial matters.

(Robert E. Lee)

TITHE TO THE SOURCES OF YOUR SPIRITUAL GROWTH

Some readers may balk at this particular principle, but it is grounded in truth. A principle of prosperity is this: True prosperity is spiritually based. I call that spiritual base God. Believing that God is the source of my prosperity, it is important to stay in touch with that Source.

In conjunction with the Law of Giving and Receiving, it is valuable to begin practicing the habit of giving back to anyone or anything that contributes to your spiritual growth. There is a wide diversity of opinion about whom to tithe to, and how much. Many claim it should all go to a church, with the most-accepted amount being ten percent (of gross or net income is another debate!). But I believe the real issue is more one of action than amount.

Become acutely aware of who touches your spirit, your soul. Pay attention to who demonstrates spiritual principles, making them come alive in your life. This is where your tithe should go.

TITHING TO A DOG?

My husband Bil says that one of his most valuable lessons in spiritual truth came from our dear little beagle, Cleo. In her old age, Cleo suffered from arthritis, making it very difficult for her to get to her favorite relaxation places — on the couch or on our bed. In the midst of this, she came down with a skin rash causing her to scratch incessantly. But even with all the difficulties, she remained patient, loving and calm. Bil said that by watching her deal with her problems, he learned important lessons about patience and trust. He tithed to Cleo by buying her a package of her favorite Jerky Treats, and making a special ceremony of giving them to her. He also designed a special ramp for her, covering it with carpet that matched our living room carpet, so she could walk up it to get to the couch or bed. Cleo was the only dog we knew with her own handicapped ramp!

Tithe to yourself as well as to your church.

(Ben Franklin)

HOW TO HANDLE COMPETITION

I'm reminded of a wonderful story that allegedly happened in New York City. There was a whole block of little independently-owned clothing stores. Suddenly, a big chain clothing outlet moved in and bought out half the block. Then, horror of horrors, a competing chain came in and bought out the other half of the block. One small store remained — smack in the middle. The owner's friends all came and begged him to sell out. "There's no way you can survive between these two giant chains. You'll go bankrupt!" they warned. But the owner insisted he'd be fine...there was plenty to go around. Well, the worst that could happen happened...*both* chains opened the same day. The owner of the small shop walked out his door and looked over to his left. He saw huge signs: **Grand Opening ... Best Prices in Town ... Everything on Sale!** When he looked toward the store on his right, again — huge signs: **Opening Week ... Two For One ... Don't Miss Out! Quality For Less Sale!**

The small shop owner was concerned — how could

he attract business when these shops had such big advertising? Then he had a brainstorm. He made *one sign* and put it right over his door — in the middle, between the new chains. It simply said: **ENTER HERE!** Now there was a man who knew how to *use* his competition to build his business.

A JOURNAL OF UNEXPECTED PROSPERITY

Keep a special Journal that is labeled "Unexpected Prosperity." In it, record all the little things that make you feel prosperous. Keep track of gifts that came from an unexpected source; money that found its way to you; an offer to buy you dinner; kind words given at just the right time. Becoming aware of all the sources from which prosperity comes can be a powerful gift in itself. And the journal is great reading in times of frustration and doubt.

 You cannot impoverish yourself by giving.

(Catherine Ponder)

IF HE'D ONLY KNOWN . . .

I'll never forget a young man I met at a National Speakers Association convention. We met at the end of the 4-day convention, while we were waiting for the van to take us to the airport. I asked him if he had enjoyed the banquet the night before, and he said, "I couldn't afford to go. I spent everything I had just to get here, and I brought stuff to eat to save money. I've eaten all my meals in my room."

I was amazed, and gasped out: "But didn't you realize that all your meals were included in your registration, including the banquet?"

The young man stared at me, incredulous. All that week he had been eating in his room, missing out on the good food, great speakers and networking opportunities available to him.

How often do we suffer when abundance is at our disposal, if we only knew it?

A Korean Legend tells of a noble warrior who died. Arriving at Heaven, he asked to see hell before entering the kingdom. His wish was granted, and to his amazement he was shown a magnificent dining room, with a huge dinner table in the center laden down with delicious food. But the inhabitants were cursing and screaming, because they were forced to eat with chopsticks that were 3 feet long. As a result, they were unable to get the food to their mouths.

On returning to heaven, the warrior discovered the exact same exquisite room, with a table laden with wonderful food. The eating implements were the same — 3 foot long chopsticks. But here, everyone was laughing and loving. The reason? These inhabitants had learned that by feeding a neighbor, they in turn would be fed.

All that we desire, all that we ever envision or hope to attain is already provided for us; it is already available and will ever be awaiting our acceptance.

(Mary Kupferle)

FROM RAGS TO RICHES

Grab a pen and notebook, and record your thoughts as you read through the next several questions. Don't censor your ideas — just write whatever comes to mind.

What would you do if you suddenly inherited a fortune? Hit the lottery? Got lucky at a casino? Think about it. What would you do if you didn't have to worry about money? What if you never had to be concerned about making financial ends meet again?

If money were no object, how would your life be different? How would you spend your wealth? Invest it? Share it? How would your superior financial status affect your attitude? Your perspective? Your health? Your friendships? What would the new richer you be like? How much money would you like to have? How would you protect your over-sized purse?

Your responses to these questions will tell you a lot about yourself, your dreams, your goals and your readiness to be suddenly rich. Review your thoughts and then ask yourself this question: What have I learned about myself . . . and what actions do I need to take next?

PRACTICE NOW

It is important to be able to handle money when it comes to you. Practice abundant living with what you have now, and demonstrate that you are a good manager of your money. It will create good habits when you have more money.

People attempt to live their lives backwards; they try to have more things, or more money, in order to do more of what they want, so they will be happier. The way it actually works is the reverse. You must first be who you really are, then do what you need to do, in order to have what you want.

(Margaret Young)

THE SOUND OF MONEY

A man and a women were walking along a crowded sidewalk in a downtown business area. Suddenly one of them exclaimed, "Did you hear the meow of that kitten?"

They both stopped and listened intently. "There it goes again. Didn't you hear it?" asked the one who heard the kitten a second time.

"How can you hear the meow of a kitten in this frenzied city?"

The companion, who was a veterinarian-turned animal rights advocate, smiled, but did not explain. She simply took a quarter out of her purse and dropped it on the sidewalk, causing a dozen people to look around for the loose change.

"We hear," she said, "what we listen for."

Listen for the sound of money and you'll hear its jingle. Listen for the still small voice and you'll experience its dividends: inner peace, happiness, thanksgiving, trust in Divine order.

FLIP A COIN!

Instead of making choices based on money, begin making your choices based on how much joy that choice will bring you. I learned a fascinating technique from my mother. When you are in the midst of a difficult decision, and cannot seem to make a firm choice, simply take out a coin. Decide which side represents which choice, then flip it in the air with gusto! When it falls, look to see which decision it selected, then immediately pay attention to how you feel inside. If you find you are saying "Yes! That's what I hoped for!" then that is the right decision; if however, you are saying "Yuk! I was afraid of this!" then go with the other option!

Nobody should be rich but those who understand it.
(Goethe)

WHY DO WE DOUBT?

I teach these prosperity principles, so I should certainly be a believer, right? But even I get surprised by the amazing way in which needs are met. In 1994, my father became ill quite suddenly and was in the hospital. I felt a very definite urge to go be with him, even though the cost of a plane ticket was going to be astronomical with the short notice. But my intuition was sending strong messages which I felt I should pay attention to. So, in spite of a meager amount of money in the checkbook, I booked Bil and I on a flight to Philadelphia, to the tune of almost $1,000.00.

Regardless of what happened next, this story is a reinforcement of how important it is to listen to our intuition. My father never left the hospital. He died within a week of our visit. Had I not gone, I never would have had the opportunity of seeing him alive and saying my good-byes to him.

But there's even more to this story! When I got my bank statement and balanced our checkbook, I discovered a subtraction error which resulted in our having — guess what — nearly $1,000.00 more money in our account that we thought! God does work in mysterious ways! This reminded me also of how we are more prosperous than outer appearances often seem. I had that money all the time, but because I couldn't see it, I didn't realize it was there. I felt poorer than I was in reality. What a wonderful metaphor for life. We are much more prosperous and successful than outer appearances sometimes reveal. Let's just believe in that truth, and feel richer than we've ever felt before!

TAKE STOCK DAILY OF YOUR PROSPERITY

At the end of each day, take time to answer this question: How am I richer than I was when I got up this morning? Include areas of health, consciousness, joy events, money, spirituality, relationship issues, and any other area of your life that contributes to your overall prosperity and inner peace. You'll discover that you are constantly adding to your prosperity consciousness.

EXPERIENCE PROSPERITY

Take advantage of opportunities to experience a level of prosperity beyond your current one. Sometimes it can be a real shock to discover the level of riches that exists in the world. On a trip to Vail, Colorado I was shopping in the little village and came upon a unique jewelry store. All the jewelry was designed and created there, and was unbelievably beautiful. I saw a gorgeous gold necklace with a huge amethyst stone in the center, that had my name written all over it! As I ogled over the necklace, the owner invited me to try it on.

You can understand my feelings, I'm sure. I hesitated, and felt instantly unworthy of even being in this expensive shop! But I decided, "What the heck? This is a great chance to taste prosperity a little." And so, I allowed him to put the necklace around my neck. Let me affirm that it was, indeed, made for me. It was fabulous! I loved it! It felt right at home there on my neck. Then I asked how much it was. He calmly replied, "$23,000.00."

That's not a typographical error! $23,000! For a necklace! It was beyond my prosperity consciousness, for sure! I looked at him and gasped: "Twenty-three THOUSAND dollars?" He immediately looked at a little notebook he held and said, "Of course, it's on sale right now for only $17,000.00."

Now, even $17,000 was way beyond anything I could imagine paying for a necklace — but I learned some very important things from that experience. I learned what really good jewelry felt like around my neck; I learned that everything can be negotiated; and I learned that there is a lot more out there than I even comprehend. By expanding my awareness, I can expand my dreams. Don't let your "Inner Pauper" keep you from experiencing life! (By the way . . . no, I did not buy the necklace! But it is forever in my memory!)

Your inner pauper...will always come up with excuses, indecisions and catastrophic expectations. No one's poverty consciousness was ever cured with a dose of money.
                                                      Jerry Gillies

CREATING JOY AND MEANING IN YOUR WORK

CREATING JOY AND MEANING IN YOUR WORK — *SNEAK PEEK*

If you suddenly became independently wealthy, what would you do? Would you keep working? In a recent survey conducted at the University of Massachusetts, an overwhelming 8 out of 10 people said YES. What the findings failed to report, but what I would like to ask is: would they continue working at their current job? My hunch would be a resounding NO.

An estimated 75% of all Americans are working at jobs they don't like...and if they had it to do all over again, they wouldn't choose their current job or employer. A Fortune study reported that of 30,000 workers interviewed, 47% dislike or at best are ambivalent about the company they work for. At the same time, another survey from Harvard indicates that U.S. wage earners are working the equivalent of an extra month of time on the job each year compared to a decade ago. Nearly half of those surveyed admitted they would willingly take less pay for more free time. We're working more now, and enjoying it less!

The reasons most people give for wanting to leave their present jobs are generally interpersonal in nature. The chief reasons are feeling unappreciated in the job; personality conflicts with their manager; stress caused by over-work and worrying about being downsized out of a job; and resentment toward management for not including them in decisions which directly affect their work. Feeling used and feeling bored are two more reasons people are dissatisfied with their work. Salary and perks are in the mix, but they are secondary to interpersonal issues.

Quality of work life is as important as the quality of work. Meaningful work is necessary for purposeful living...because work is an extension of who we are. Peter Senge said: "People shouldn't have to leave their jobs to find one that's more meaningful. Many can find meaning if they just think about their jobs differently." This section takes a look at the impact of your work on your life, and gives you tools to discover joy and meaning in the work you do.

If you are unhappy in the work you do, it drains you of energy and builds a negative attitude that infects everything else you do. By applying the principles and strategies in this section, you can take charge of your feelings about your work, and move toward doing the work you were put here to do. When you are using your skills and talents to contribute to the world in your own special, unique way, you will feel a continual flow of energy, power and enthusiasm. If you currently dislike your job, this section will help you "love your way out of it." If you aren't sure of what your life purpose really is, you'll find tools to help you discover it.

When you have joy and meaning in the work you do, you experience a strong sense of inner peace that sustains you when you run into problems and challenges. You can cope with every other area of your life more effectively when your work is consistent with your values, your interests and your goals. Have fun exploring this section to discover joy and meaning in the work you do.

DO WHAT YOU LOVE

I asked people who loved their work to tell me why they loved it. Despite the diversity of the people I interviewed and the wide-variety of professions and types of work represented, people had two things in common. They loved their work because they considered it meaningful and because they felt fulfilled.

In every case, these people are unwilling to structure their lives according to the standards of others. People who love what they do unanimously said they do not seek the approval of others for their chosen line of work. Pay is not a prime motivation, and neither is job title or position.

Their sense of self-worth isn't identified with work. They feel good about themselves because the work they do is an extension of their values and beliefs. Their parameters as human beings far exceed the boundaries of work, making them whole people, people who love work but keep it in perspective.

COLOR OUTSIDE THE LINES!

Sales Rep.: How can I stretch myself? Expand my horizons? I'm stuck in a nowhere job in a nowhere industry.

Cher: Color inside the lines to please convention. Color outside the lines to honor your individuality. Do what you must to function in your job, but look for ways to bring fun into your work. Focus on the joy of the work, and try new things (or do old things in new ways). You'll find that you color yourself right out of your ruts, and into a whole new coloring book!

FIND FUN!

Fun helps remove the barriers that allow people to motivate themselves. Look for ways to have more fun at work.

WHY DO I DO THIS?

Tom Malone, President of Milliken & Co., remembers playing football in college. By his own admission, he wasn't very big, and he wasn't very good. He got hurt a lot, including a broken arm, broken neck, and six broken noses! People always asked him why he kept doing it. His reply: "If there hadn't been any fans in the stands

cheering me on — my family and friends — I wouldn't
have kept on playing and trying so hard. But there were,
so I did." (*The Motivational Manager*)

HITTING THE 'SARAN WRAP WALL'

We rarely have the luxury of choosing who we get
to work with, but we can choose who we share our goals
with. As you move toward the work of your dreams, be
sure you are sharing those dreams with people who support you and believe you can achieve those goals. Too
often, we find ourselves running smack into what I call
the 'Saran Wrap Wall'. The 'Saran Wrap Wall' is that
invisible wall constructed by well-meaning friends and
colleagues who say things like: "Why can't you be satisfied with what you have?", "What's gotten into you —
thinking you can do something like that?", or "You used
to be more fun before you became such a workaholic."

These so-called friends claim to support us, then
send messages that damage our self-esteem, smash our
faith in ourselves, and drain our energy and enthusiasm.
It's dangerous because, like saran wrap, the effects are
difficult to see, yet wrap around our dreams so tightly
they cannot breathe.

Cut through that 'Saran Wrap Wall' by taking a
strong stand for your dreams! Then choose to share
those dreams only with people who are willing to support you in achieving them. As for the others, just thank
them for their input, and let them go.

Invent your world. Surround yourself with people, color,
sounds, and work that nourish you.

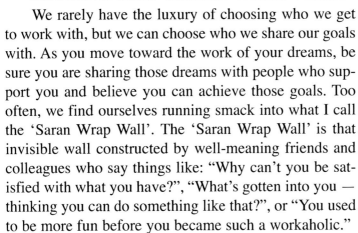

(*Sark*)

FOCUS ON THE POSITIVE

No matter what job you are doing right now, you can enjoy it more. Make a conscious decision to focus on what parts of your job bring you joy. What skills do you have an opportunity to use? How are you contributing to helping others, and bringing joy and harmony into your workplace? As you change your focus, you will discover that your job takes on a whole new dimension, and you take on a new radiance.

WHAT DO YOU ENJOY?

Spend some time with your Self-Development Notebook and pen, jotting down answers to the following questions.

- What are five things I really enjoy doing?
- What are my five strongest skills and/or talents?
- What kind of people do I prefer to be with, and why?
- What kinds of books and magazines do I enjoy reading in my spare time?
- What are my hobbies and fun activities?

Take a look at your responses, and then assess what they tell you about the work you should be doing. Are there ways you can bring what you enjoy into what you do for a living? How can you make better use of your talents and skills? How can you attract more of the kinds of people you enjoy into your work? Are there ways you can do something 'on the side' to test the waters for a future life work?

Try not to get too caught up in how much money you could make, or what the barriers might be. This is a time to let your thoughts flow, and attract ideas to move closer to a job you can truly enjoy.

If you are not having fun in your work, you're paying too high a price!

LEARN FROM THE TRASH CAN

Suppose you are meeting with a few colleagues in a conference room. Your absorbing conversation is interrupted by the sound of metal ricocheting off wood, followed by a human cry. When you glance in the direction of the commotion, you see that a co-worker entering the room has just tripped over a metal trash can. The embarrassed colleague picks up the trash can, apologizes and politely seats himself.

What's your immediate impression of the co-worker? Klutz? Bungler? Clumsy oaf?

Okay, five minutes later someone else walks into the conference room and she, too, trips over the trash can. Ten minutes later another person stumbles over the same trash can.

What's your opinion now? Maybe the trash can's in the wrong place. Perhaps the last person didn't put it far enough out of the way. Or maybe the room is too small. In any case, the trash can is the problem, not the person.

How often do we complain about the wrong things, and focus on a symptom rather than a cause? The next time you make an assumption, base it on fact, not conjecture. Hesitate before you assign blame too quickly. It may be an out-of-place rule, policy, procedure, belief, law and so on. Be sure you're focusing on the trash can.

THE "LIFESTYLE" PRINCIPLE

As you begin to redefine your work, keep this principle in mind: *First determine the kind of lifestyle you want, then wrap your work around that lifestyle.*

Think about what this means. If your lifestyle calls for lots of family time, then you certainly don't want to accept the promotion that will force you to travel three weeks out of every month. If money is a critical part of your lifestyle needs, then you might be wise to accept the offer of time-and-a-half and work the holiday weekend. Once you know WHAT you want, the HOW becomes much easier to determine.

HIGH TECH/HIGH TOUCH

Telecommunications Team Leader: Cher, what you said about technology and touch this morning has haunted me all day. Our lives are so busy . . . and technology does make it easier. How can I make time to get more "high touch" in my "high-tech" world?

Cher: The very fact that you're asking the question means you're aware of how important it is. That's great! Try this: Every time you start to send an email to someone, ask yourself if it might be more appropriate to call or go see the person, and *tell* them what you want to say. Another idea: Carry ten pennies in your right pocket. Your daily goal is to move the ten pennies from your right pocket to your left pocket. The way a penny gets moved is by talking face-to-face with a person on a non-job related topic. Just be sure you don't spend the pennies before they get moved!

A STRONG SENSE OF VISION

In a study published in *Reinventing the CEO,* 1989, the behavioral trait most frequently mentioned as desirable in CEO's by over 1,500 leaders from twenty different countries is a strong sense of vision of the future. Do you know what you want your work to look like a year from now? Five years? Twenty?

FAST FORWARD

Mentally fast forward to a year from now. In the

best of all possible worlds, what are you doing? Vividly describe it in your Self-Development Notebook. Be specific. Do it again for five years from now. Then answer one question: What could I do right now, where I am with what I have, to move me at least a baby-step closer to that vision? Then — do it!

HONEST WORK

Restaurant Manager: These kids think this work is degrading, but they don't have the skills to do anything else. How can I help them feel better about what they are doing?

Cher: People who consider their work beneath them generally are above doing any of it well. Honest work is never degrading. Take time to emphasize the value of what each person is doing, and how important it is to the success of your restaurant. Offer ways for them to develop additional skills. Listen to them. And above all else, thank them.

Let us stop equating work with earning a living, but rather think of it as an important component of making a life.
(R.C. Weinrich, from Michigan Business Review)

CELEBRATE ACHIEVEMENT

Find at least one tiny event to celebrate each week. It can be someone's birthday, wedding anniversary, educational achievement or work accomplishment. The mini-celebration doesn't have to be lavish or over-done. It can be a box of candy, a package of cookies, a good book (this one would make a terrific gift), balloons, flowers, or simply applause.

Hold the appreciation celebration at the person's

work station or nearby area in full view of admiring peers. Ceremoniously lead the group in a cheer or standing ovation. This simple, thoughtful, gesture will make a world of difference in team spirit, morale, and — believe it or not — productivity. And you'll get a reputation as a person who knows how to make other people feel terrific!

A job is what we do for money; work is what we do for love.

(Marysarah Quinn)

ROUTINE ROUTINES

Product Engineer: I've been routinized to death, Cher. I'm in a rut and it's making me hate coming to work. What can I do?

Cher: First realize that all routines aren't bad. The trick is to modify or eliminate non-productive and irrelevant routines. Some routines — like eating, exercising, saving money, praying, driving to work — are essential. Others get in our way, and can actually make our work more difficult. I'd recommend that you take a close look at the routines you have in your life, particularly at work. Live with those that serve your values and beliefs and bottom lines. Leave the ones that dull your senses, stifle creativity, drain your energy, or remove the joy you feel about what you're doing. And try to do something routine in a totally different way — for instance, try having your next staff meeting outdoors!

Without work, all life goes rotten. But when work is soulless, life stifles and dies.

(Albert Camus)

FOLLOW YOUR OWN LEAD

Senior Executive V.P. of Marketing: Sometimes, Cher, I just want to walk away from these responsibilities — to take this job and shove it! What can I do?

Cher: It's vitally important to find meaningful work. Otherwise we have difficulty turning off the internal alarm which says, "Get out of here. Run, don't walk!"

Marketing V.P.: That's exactly how I feel ... like running. Running away. Should I?

Cher: Well, maybe not run away. But it is important to let the frustrated, restless, doubtful, angry, disenchanted, over-worked you out. You won't have to run far. Just find a quiet place and sit. Ask your wiser self what work you should do, and then listen. Repeat this process until you find an answer. Then follow your own lead.

THE MESSAGE OF THE GOLF TEES

One of the saddest stories I've heard came from a woman in one of my audiences. After my keynote, she came up to me with tears in her eyes and said, "Cher, what you said about taking time to enjoy life — it is so true! My husband recently died of a heart attack, right in the office. When I went in and cleaned out his desk, in the drawer I found golf tees, along with a note he'd written to himself. It said, 'Someday I want to go out and play golf again!' He'd given up his fun for that job, thinking he had plenty of time later for stuff like golf — and dreams — and his own business. He put it all on hold, to make the big bucks quickly by selling his soul to that company. I had those golf tees and his note framed, and I keep it on my desk to remind myself to take time now for the fun."

I'm not sure I'd want the tees and that note as a constant reminder of the sadness, but the message is certainly poignant and clear.

 Work and play are the same. When you're following your energy and doing what you want all the time, the distinction between work and play dissolves.

(Shakti Gawain)

OBSOLETE 40-HOUR WORKWEEK

Research conducted by the U.S. Labor Department found that, for both genders and in every age category, the number of people working 49 or more hours per week has increased, making the 40-hour standard workweek established 60 years ago obsolete.

STRETCHING TOWARD THE GOAL

In my workshops, I often use a visual prop to help audiences grasp a concept I am sharing. Imagine you are holding a very large rubber band, or perhaps one of those exercise stretch bands. As you grasp it with both hands, begin pulling your hands apart, with your right hand moving upward and your left hand moving downward. Pull until you cannot stretch it anymore.

Now, imagine that the upper portion represents your work goal — the desired job or career you have envisioned. The lower portion represents your current state — where you are right now. The gap stretching between them is very uncomfortable, right? It creates a tension that becomes almost unbearable.

Too often, the way we relieve that stress and tension is to move the upper portion downward. We lower our expectations, put brakes on our dreams, and settle for less than we wanted. Sure, it's more comfortable. But how do we feel inside? What have we sacrificed for our comfort? And how long will we be satisfied with this particular comfort zone?

How much better to relieve that tension by moving the lower portion closer to the top. Take small steps toward the goal or dream. Each little step lessens the gap. Keep the dream locked in, and move ever so much closer with every action. The tension is still being relieved, and you have created a strong singleness of purpose focusing on the vision of your perfect work.

Life is to be lived. If you have to support yourself, you had bloody well better find some way that is going to be interesting.

(Katharine Hepburn)

According to a survey , 40% of newly promoted managers fail. The primary reason: failure to build partnerships and team work with subordinates and peers.

WHO DO I WANT TO BE?

Many years ago, when I was a secretary with the  U.S. Postal Service, I attended a half-day career development workshop. One of the activities invited us to imagine we were 100 years old, being interviewed by a newspaper reporter. The question was: What accomplishments are you most proud of? One of the things I wrote down as a response was: "I had my own business, training and sharing with people how to improve their life."

This was so far from what I was actually doing that I was embarrassed even to show it to people. But the idea stuck in my mind. The goal intrigued me. It grew as I focused on it, and began to research how to go about achieving it. I talked with people, explored the possibilities and looked for opportunities to learn about the fields I could enter. On my job, I began to take on additional responsibilities that gave me skills in that area. My coworkers thought I was crazy to do extra work with no extra pay. They didn't realize that I was working toward my vision.

It didn't happen overnight by any means, and it required a lot of effort and commitment, but isn't it interesting that I now have my own business, and I provide consulting, training and keynote speeches to individuals and corporations throughout the country, helping them improve their work and their lives? Having that vision is a critical first step toward your future happiness and inner peace.

THERE FROM HERE

Marketing Manager: What I'm doing is so far away from what I want to do, that I want to scream sometimes.

Cher: What do you want to do? What brings you joy and satisfaction?

Marketing Manager: It's got nothing to do with this place. I'd love to own and operate a gourmet coffee shop.

Cher: I'd like to be your first customer.

Marketing Manager: Great! So, how do I get there from here?

Cher: First, you accept that it is natural to want something more than what you are experiencing. Swiss psychologist Carl Jung talked about synchronicity, which means a fortuitous intermeshing of events.

Some folks call it coincidence, or serendipity. What it means is — your desire to do what you feel led to do will set in motion fortuitous events which will bring you the essence of what you want.

Marketing Manager: What you're saying is giving me hope. What do you mean it'll bring me the essence of what I want?

Cher: Your dissatisfaction with where you are is prompting you to change. Ask yourself, what does the essence of owning a coffee shop mean? How do I feel when I drink coffee? What affect does drinking coffee — gourmet coffee — have on me, psychologically, emotionally, physically? Why coffee? Why not tea, or pizza, or automobiles? How can I get that essence on my job right now? And what can I do that is one small step towards where I want to go? Trust the process. It'll bring you what's good for you.

If you aren't having fun in your work, fix the problem *before it becomes serious. Ask for help if you need it. If you can't fix it and won't ask for help, please go away before you spoil the fun for the rest of us.*

(Russ Walden)

BOOK REVIEW

Invite your colleagues to organize a book-of-the-month club. Select a book on a topic of interest to the group. Agree to read the book in its entirety (or selected chapters if reading the whole book is overwhelming!). Jot down comments, highlight significant concepts or advice, and underline important content.

At an agreed-upon time, get together to discuss the book (or chapters) and share insights. Identify how the book's content relates to your specific work situation and how you can make improvements based on what you've read.

I've seen this technique literally transform not only individuals, but organizations. People get excited when they talk about good ideas, especially when the proposed idea is relevant to the work they do.

Be your own internal consultants on certain issues, using the book as your guide. This technique is simple, cost effective and surprisingly manageable.

 I suggest that the only books that influence us are those for which we are ready, and which have gone a little farther down our particular path than we have gone ourselves.

(E.M. Foster)

CREATE A "STRESS-FREE" ZONE

Designate a specific area as a Stress-Free Zone. When you are there, no one can interrupt you or disturb you. I've seen companies who allow employees to design their own zones, with permission to spend a maximum of 15 minutes there at their own discretion. One area had a small rug, a rocking chair, and a CD player with headphones. Another had a hammock stretched catty-cornered, with a fake palm tree, magazines and a small refrigerator. Another company set up a miniature golf course in the hallway and through the cubicles — after hours, of course. What's interesting is that nowhere this idea is used has it been abused by employees. So — set up your Stress-Free Zone, and take time out to relax!

 We need to reorient our thinking so that we can realistically feel we are leading successful lives right now, without having to earn any more money, buy any more stuff, or reach any new heights.

(Steven Carter & Julia Sokol, Lives Without Balance)

HOW TO LEARN A NEW SKILL

If you want to be a pro at something, find someone who is already a pro at it and ask if you can pick up a few tricks of the trade. The world is full of folks who do things well and are more than willing to share their knowledge with others.

MEET THE PRO

Schedule a time when you can view the pro in action. Watch how the pro handles your targeted skill. Focus on how he or she creates the magic in your area of interest. Take copious notes. If possible, meet with the pro to debrief your observations. Practice what you've learned, assess your progress and reschedule a visit with your pro to critique your progress. Test your skill, re-evaluate it with your pro, and test your ability again.

After the initial supervised runs, test and monitor your own progress for a while before you ask for more input from your busy pro. Inform the pro of your progress. Demonstrate your newly-acquired skill, if it's possible. Be open to additional feedback. Polish your newly-developed skill. Own it. Honor it.

By the way, don't forget to say thank-you to the pro who has helped you! And be ready and willing to serve as a pro to someone else coming along who can learn something from you.

If one is master of one thing and understands one thing well, one has at the same time insight into and understanding of many things.

(Vincent Van Gogh)

> **"I Love My Job!"** 1984 Olympic Gold medalist
> Scott Hamilton, when interviewed after his successful
> fight against testicular cancer, said, "I want to retire
> on my terms. I don't want this episode to stop me
> from skating. When I no longer enjoy it, I will stop. I
> love my job, and that is inspiration enough."
> (*Associated Press*, April, 1997)

PEERING AT RETIREMENT

During a recent speaking engagement, I was
approached by one of the key meeting planners in the
company. He announced rather sadly that in one year,
he'd be retiring and that it had never occurred to him
what he would do after he retired. He admitted he was
afraid; he didn't know what he was going to do with the
extra time. By his own admission, his wife and grown
children were just as concerned about his post retirement
years.

We talked about a few of his ideas and retirement
pursuits, including his being asked to work for the company as a consultant for a year. He brightened when he
mentioned this, but I noticed a hint of reticence in his
cheerful expression. He seemed unsure of himself,
uncertain about the rest of his life.

I counseled him as best I could. He thanked me for
my advice. He said I really helped him. But as I watched
him walk quickly up the aisle, I realized he was the
teacher and I was the student. The purpose of our brief
encounter was to remind me that so many of us identify
our whole being, our sense of self-worth with the work
we do. Much of our value, as a productive human being,
is imbedded in work. And so some people believe that
when they retire, they lose their value. They believe their
worth is diminished somehow.

I reaffirmed to myself that our value is in who we are, and not what we do. Work is only one of the expressions of how we choose to spend our time. We are more, much more that where we live, how we dress and what we do for a living.

RETIRE? NEVER!

In an interview, Charles Schultz, creator of the famous Peanuts comic strip, was asked if he ever was able to get ahead on his comic strip so he could take a long break. He looked confused, then responded: "You don't work all your life to get to do something so you don't have to do it." (*Raleigh N&O*)

There are few failures among people who have found work they like enough to do well.

(Clarence Flynn)

WHY AM I STUCK IN THIS JOB?

Administrative Assistant: Cher, what you've said makes sense, and I promise, if I had a job I enjoyed more, I could be more positive. So, why am I stuck in this stupid job where I'm not appreciated and don't get to use my skills?

Cher: It's obvious you're not happy where you are. But one thing I've learned — and you probably won't want to hear this — is that we're put in situations because we have something we need to learn. So, you might ask yourself what lessons you can learn from this particular job. Perhaps it's humility, or initiative from within, or maybe developing skills in dealing with difficult people. Or maybe it's to understand the value of appreciation — something you'll need for your future work.

One thing is for sure — the faster we learn our lessons, the faster we get to move on! So why not start focusing on the joy you can find in the work you do, and "learn" your way out of the current situation?

Your real work lies in a straight line before you. A new opportunity will open whenever you have gained all the discipline and knowledge that the old work has to offer you. Meanwhile, remind yourself that there is no work that is high or low, so long as it is essential to the welfare of anyone.

(Catherine Ponder)

Money is an excellent servant, but a terrible master.

(P. T. Barnum)

Nobody ever drowned in his own sweat.

(Ann Landers)

PERSIST IN THE WORK YOU LOVE

Michael Flatley became a star the old-fashioned way: he earned it! Michael is the creator and star of the popular "Lord of the Dance" — but it didn't come easy. He says he always wanted to create, and to dance. And he had the talent. At 17 he became the first non-European to win the World Irish Dance Championship in Dublin. His feet have been clocked at 28 taps per second! But for all his talent, he was unable to support himself as a dancer. His closest friends and his family all urged him to get out of dance, and get into a lucrative business of some sort. But he persevered, and it paid off. His show has grossed more than $100 million, and he has tens of thousands of fans around the world.

I can't guarantee that if you do what you love, the

money will follow. But I can guarantee that if you do what you love, the money won't be as important to you. The sense of inner peace and fulfillment you receive will give you far more than money you get from doing a job in which you aren't happy. Listen to your inner wisdom, and persevere in the work that you love.

EDIBLE PLAY DOUGH: Exercise your creativity by trying the art of edible play dough. Identify the work-related problem that is mystifying you. Ask you inner guidance to give you ideas for solutions. Then, go to work playing with the play dough (recipe below). Let yourself go as you mold the play dough into a solution. Or, create with the play dough some representation of your problem, then eat it! It's great symbolism for taking control over your problems!

Recipe for Edible Play Dough: Mix together 18 oz. of peanut butter, 6 Tbsp. honey, and enough non-fat dry milk to create the right consistency. You can add cocoa or carob for flavor, and vanilla or almond drops to create a pleasant scent. Enjoy!

'DOWNSHIFTING'

As many as 25% of Americans will strive to scale back their lives to some degree in the next ten years, according to the Trends Research Institute. Consultants who once coached professionals on how to get ahead are now giving advice on ways to 'downshift'. A 1997 study by Minneapolis-based Lutheran Brotherhood found 32% of participants would give up their lifestyle in exchange for a simpler one with less pay. (*USA Today*, 04/09/98)

One of the saddest experiences which can come to human beings is to awaken, gray-haired and wrinkled, near the close of an unproductive career, to the fact that all through the years they have been using only a small part of themselves.

(V. B. Burrows)

FIVE ACTIONS TO TAKE BEFORE YOU 'DOWNSHIFT'

If you're thinking of taking the 'downshifting' route to bring some meaning to your life or to leave the corporate world behind in favor of working for yourself, consider taking these five actions before making the move, to up your chances for success.

- *Remove your financial blinders.* Get out of debt. Practice living on less, while you stash the unused money into a separate account. You should have a minimum of six months living expenses saved before you consider leaving your current situation.
- *Develop a realistic plan of action.* If you'll have more time, but less money, how do you plan to spend the time without going into debt? If you're starting your own business, develop your business plan. Be clear about what is going to happen once you make the change.
- *Have a good talk with your ego.* 'Downshifters' take a lot of heat from family and friends about their decision. Can your ego handle the potential loss of status and financial security?
- *Have a good talk with your 'significant others.'* Remember that you are not the only one who will be affected by the change. What impact will it have on your spouse, your children, others who are close to you? How will it affect your lifestyle, vacations, free

time, recreation, etc.? Is everyone willing and able to make the sacrifices? Are the sacrifices worth the return?

- *Get real!* Be sure you know what you're getting into [as much as you can]. Talk to others who have already 'been there, done that.' Read books about it. Learn as much as you can, so you can make an educated decision. Then — Go For It!

MAKE YOUR JOB EXCITING!

If you travel at all, you've probably experienced a shuttle ride from the airport to your hotel. Typically it is a pretty grim trip, with weary travelers wearing a glazed-over look in their eyes, and the driver speaking only when someone ventures to ask a question. But in Raleigh, NC there was a shuttle driver named Dan Young who made a choice about his job. He chose to be unique — and make his job fun.

Once the shuttle is underway, he treats his customers to a one-man show! Throughout the shuttle ride, he takes on the persona of Augustus Young, H-E-R-T-Z Radio. Between terminal stops and the rental car office, he provides his passengers with a running commentary of games, poems and jokes, advice on restaurants and tourist attractions, and recounts significant events at the airport. He also conducts interviews with the stars — all of whom Dan sits in for. Dan says: "Don't look for us on your AM/FM band. We don't have a very strong signal. We only play to captive audiences!"

To love what you do and feel that it matters — how can anything be more fun?

(*Katharine Graham*)

ENRICHING INTERPERSONAL RELATIONSHIPS

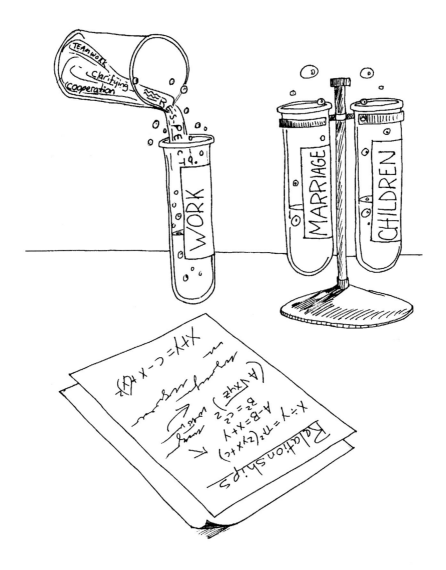

ENRICHING INTERPERSONAL
RELATIONSHIPS — *SNEAK PEEK*

An ancient story is told of three brothers who were traveling by horseback across the country. Every evening, as the sun set on the horizon, they would stop wherever they were and set up camp for the night.

One evening, as the sun was casting rays of red, purple and gold across the sky, the brothers found themselves at the side of a beautiful lake. Deciding this was a perfect spot to sleep for the night, they began to unload. Suddenly, they heard a voice speak out of nowhere: "Listen to me, and do as I say."

The brothers looked at each other, each fearing the others had not heard anything and would think him mad. But it was obvious from their expressions that they had all heard the voice. Then, it echoed again: "Listen to me and do as I say. Gather as many stones as you can up from the lakeside and put them in your saddlebags. Do not look in your saddlebags again until you reach tomorrow night's destination. Then you will discover this has been your most exciting moment — and your most frustrating moment."

As the voice stilled, the brothers excitedly discussed the implications. They agreed it was worth doing, and began to gather stones. But as they realized the heavy weight of those stones they would be carrying the entire next day, their enthusiasm waned. Each selected only a few stones, which got stowed away in the saddlebags. Then they went to sleep.

The next morning they were off, anxious to peek into their saddlebags, but staying obedient to the voice's instructions. That evening, as they unloaded their bags, the brothers were astounded to discover that the stones had turned to gold. Excitedly they counted out their treasure, and one brother cried, "This is definitely the most exciting moment in our lives!"

But then the oldest brother solemnly looked at his siblings and said, "No, this is the most frustrating moment of our lives. Just imagine what treasure we could have right now, if only we had been willing to carry a little more weight through the day."

The lesson learned by these brothers is a lesson for us in terms of our interpersonal relationships. Dealing with other people can truly be the most exciting experience in our life. People are very important to us. When successful individuals are interviewed, they invariably mention that they could not have achieved their success without the help of others. When football players find themselves in front of a camera, they cannot resist the temptation to mouth the words, "Hi, Mom!" And how many of you, like me, cry during the Hallmark Card commercials, because they truly touch at the very heart of our relationships with others?

But there is a flip side. Any time you have to interact with another person, it has the potential to be the most frustrating experience of your life! No matter who you are, no matter what you do, you may find yourself involved in many different conflict situations with "difficult people." These conflicts take on many forms: disagreements . . . misunderstandings . . . stubbornness . . . resentment . . . anger . . . criticism . . . intimidation . . . value differences . . . negative attitudes . . . betrayals . . . and the list goes on. Business success, fulfilling marriages, friendships and community involvements all depend on people working together — and that demands skill.

Of course, the "Reality Factor" confirms that there are some people who just don't want to cooperate. I call these the "two per-centers," because research says there are about 2% of the folks you deal with who fall in this category. When you do something to make them happy, they are even more upset because they do not want to be happy! With these two per-centers, you just have to do the best you can, then release them to their highest good and move on.

With the other 98%, there is a secret. It's the lesson learned by the brothers in our story. You can enjoy more fulfilling, enriching relationships with others if you are willing to take on a little more than your share of the weight — the responsibility — in making the relationship work.

This dynamic chapter is designed to help you strengthen your interpersonal skills so you can work with others more effectively — with everyone feeling good about the results. Every principle, quote, story, and activity reiterates the message. It is not the other person who will change. It is your initiative, your action, your inner growth that will make the difference. So, read through this chapter and choose the ideas that make sense to you. The payoff is a tremendous improvement in your interpersonal relationships, and an inner peace that comes from knowing how to transform any interaction into a positive experience.

I'D LOVE TO

In the following categories, record your thoughts as quickly as you can. Do not censor your answers or think about them too long. Just answer . . . and trust me!

Think about someone who is special to you.

I'd love to take that person _____
_____

I'd love to buy that person _____
_____

I'd love to tell that person _____
_____

I'd love for that person to _____

_____

I'd love to admit to that person _____

_____

I'd love, for that person's sake, to _____

_____

I'd love to send that person _____

_____

I'd love to give that person _____

_____

Continue with this activity, using the same questions but filling in other people who are important to you. For example, my spouse; my children; my parent(s); my in-laws; my boss; my neighbor; my brother or sister; an old friend you haven't seen for a long time; etc.

Now, review your responses and listen to what they tell you. Is there anything you can do right now? What's preventing you? If it's money, can you capture the *essence* of the idea in some other way? Are there any patterns in your responses?

Decide on one thing you can do immediately to make one of your "I'd love to's" a reality. Now, do it! Experience the difference you can make, by taking one small action. Do this activity often, and reap the benefits of renewed joy in your relationships with those who are important to you.

Whenever two people meet, there are really six present. There is each man as he sees himself, each as the other person sees him and each man as he really is.
                              (William James)

CRAZYMAKERS

In her book, *The Artist's Way*, Julia Cameron refers to 'Crazymakers" — individuals who create storm centers wherever they go. They love drama, and if allowed, will take over everyone else's life so it revolves around theirs. These are the people who pit one person against another; expect special treatment; are inconsiderate of your time and resources; bring 'emergencies' to your planned schedule; and fail to adhere to commitments they have made.

If crazymakers are preventing you from finding fulfillment in your work (or your life), it's time to take control of them. First, identify who they are. This makes it easier for you to recognize their games. Then, set limits and stick by them. Consider your priorities as important as theirs. Clarify your expectations, and require commitments to be followed through on. If all else fails, ask yourself what personal benefits you get from your involvement with this crazymaker. Then ask yourself if the benefits are worth it.

 The meeting of two personalities is like the content of two chemical substances; if there is any reaction, both are transformed.

(Carl Jung)

BE FIRST

In any situation involving another person, make it a game with yourself to be the first one to make a positive contribution to the relationship. Whether it is to make eye contact, to smile, to apologize, to initiate an activity, to compliment, to lend an ear to listen or shoulder to cry on, to offer assistance, to just 'be there', make it a point to be a doer, not a waiter. Too many people wait for someone else to take the first step, and as a result live a life a lonely desperation.

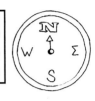

> **PRINCIPLE OF APPRECIATION:** People who feel appreciated and trusted will push themselves to achieve extraordinary results.

BENCH-SITTING CYNICISM

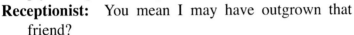

Receptionist: What do I tell a friend who says I'm totally different than I used to be?

Cher: Beware of subtle sabotage from friends. Be particularly alert for any suggestion from a jealous friend who accuses you of being selfish or different or not the same person you used to be. It may simply be a question of growth and maturation.

Receptionist: You mean I may have outgrown that friend?

Cher: Perhaps. I'd need to know more about your relationship, but from what you've told me, the overtones from your friend may be attempts to slow your advance and pull you back toward the old, more predictable you. Your growth may be pushing your friend outside her comfort zone and threatening her. Blocked friends may find your energy and enthusiasm for change a bit disturbing. Please don't allow their bench-sitting cynicism or their fears and doubts to derail you.

JUST SAY THANKS

For one week, monitor how many times you either refused to accept or begrudgingly accepted gifts, compliments or help. (For example: "You look terrific" — *Oh, do you really think so? I've been under the weather;* "I'll clean that for you." — *That's okay, I can get it;* "Here, I baked this for you." *You didn't have to do that;* "You've helped me enough times, I thought I'd return the favor." — *I don't expect you to help me, but as long*

as you're here; "I bought this for you." *Why you little spendthrift. I told you I didn't need anything.)*

Start saying *thank you,* instead of launching one of your objections. That's right — a simple series of two words: thank you. Let people know how much you appreciate their thoughtfulness. It's their way of investing in the relationship, so use the currency of *thank you's* to tip their kindness.

THE INNER CIRCLE

Draw a circle on a sheet of paper. It should be at least six inches in diameter. Now think of friends, work associates, family who nurture you (give you a sense of your own competence and self-worth and future success). Write their names inside the circle.

Think of other people who repeatedly suggest that you either can't or shouldn't do something without their help or some kind of miracle. Write their names outside the circle.

Use a pair of scissors to cut the circle out of the page. Throw your detractors (the people outside the circle) in the nearest trash can. Paste the inner circle on another sheet of paper and record anything you can remember about how your nurturers have described you. Also list the qualities you admire in your nurturers.

Review your list. Accept the praise and compliments you've gotten. Realize that the qualities you admire in your inner circle of nurturers are the same qualities you possess to some degree. Like attracts like. Begin expressing those qualities that you admire as a part of the new you. It's always been there. Your nurturers have sensed it.

STRAIGHT FROM THE
DOCTOR'S MOUTH

Mandy Patinkin, who played Dr. Jeffrey Geiger on the T.V. show Chicago Hope, made a powerful observation. In preparing for his role, he viewed 16 open heart surgeries. His awareness: "I've seen every sex, every size, every ethnicity on the table and inside, they were all identical. The irony is that inside we're made the same, but something on the outside makes us all so different."

Let's focus on how we are similar to others, then move on to honoring and appreciating the differences that make us unique.

A successful person is one who can lay a firm foundation with the bricks that others throw at him(/her).

(David Brinkley)

REOPENING ROCKY ROADS

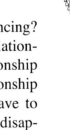

Pick one or two rocky interpersonal relationships (i.e. family member, friend, co-worker, former spouse, community service or club associate). Review, in your own mind, the circumstances leading to the split.

What factors led to your interpersonal distancing? What caused the process of disengagement, of relationship decay? When did the embattered relationship dissolve? Who destroyed it? Could the relationship move from desolation to repair? What would have to happen to help you move beyond the pain and disappointment? How could you move closer to some type of reconciliation? Is reconciliation possible? Or wanted?

Study the rift again. Review the trail of tears and anger. Place the past under your *emotional microscope.* Examine every slight and shadow, each nostalgic coral reef, every memorable tense moment. Inspect each instance of emotional piracy or toneless conversation. Determine when each of you became devoid of empathy and settled for a robotic, uncaring relationship.

Consider repairing the strained relationship. Start with forgiveness. What can you do to move the dysfunctional relationship toward a personally satisfactory, if not mutually satisfying outcome? Maybe you've done all you can. Maybe you haven't. If you can't handle the repair alone, ask for help (close friend, family, therapist). Do the right thing for the right reasons. But whatever you choose to do, move toward a more complete, happier, healthier personhood.

The ability to resign, to let go of obsolete responses, of exhausted relationships and of tasks beyond one's potential is an essential part of the wisdom of living.

(Frederick S. Perls)

TRENDS

Trends is another way of saying change. And change strikes fear in the hearts of many people. Change disrupts the status quo. It involves repatterning. It brings unknown challenges. Worrisome risks. Assaults on protective egos. It devours outdated procedures, submarines timidity and indecisiveness, and chisels away at proven track records and mindless convention. It forces growth or demise, movement or stagnation, success or failure. And it can play havoc with relationships.

Think back on your past relationships, and identify how change has affected them. Look for the trends that are in your life right now, redefining who you are and how you interact with those around you. As you learn to recognize the trends that bring change into your life, you are better able to prepare for and welcome it. Run freely beside it like children who roll a tire down the street. Trends, like tires, are easier to handle in the direction they're headed.

LIKE ATTRACTS LIKE

This is not easy to swallow, but I encourage you to give it some thought. What disturbs or bothers us most about another person is actually a mirror reflecting back something about ourselves we need to learn. It doesn't necessarily mean we have that trait, but it may mean we attract that trait to us in some way. Or perhaps we express it in another way.

Emmet Fox explained it this way: "If you came to me and told me that you can't get along with people, I should tell you to get a card about the size of a postcard and write this on it: 'Like attracts like…' People come to me and say: 'If you only knew the kind of people I have to be with and work with!' I say, The Law of Being says, *like attracts like.*"

SURROUND YOURSELF WITH MASTER ENERGIZERS

Business Owner: Cher, when I get depressed, my friends all commiserate with me, and it turns into a gigantic pity party that leaves me feeling worse instead of better. How can I get out of this rut?

Cher: Surround yourself with people who are master *energizers* — who believe in you and want to see you succeed. These catalysts are people who have the uncanny ability to move you toward unbeliev- able excellence, who consistently and with immense pride empower you to out-perform yourself. Use these people as barometers. Accept their encourage- ment and advice as "I can do it" manna.

Business Owner: It's hard for me to ask for help. I don't want people to think I'm whining.

C   h   e   r   :
There's a big difference between whining and asking for help . . . even in the tone of voice as you speak. The secret lies in your receptivity. If you ask someone for advice or help, listen to their ideas. Avoid second-guessing them, or playing 'yes, but' games by explaining why something won't work. Master energizers have a zest for life that is contagious. Catch it!

Don't suffer from a 'pain in the ask!

NOTHING SAYS LOVIN' LIKE SOME-THING FROM THE OVEN: According to Futurist Magazine, we should fill the air with scents of cookies and coffee to make the world a nicer place. In experiments at a mall, strangers were more willing to help one another when exposed to pleasant aromas. Passersby were more than twice as likely to retrieve a dropped pen or provide change for a dollar when they could smell cookies baking or coffee roasting.

QUIT WHINING!

I had a lesson about whining hit me right between the eyes. It made me realize that we aren't always aware of how we sound to others. In one of my dance lessons, I was feeling particularly vulnerable about my lack of poise and grace on the dance floor. In trying to apologize to Robert, my instructor, for my klutziness, I kept saying "I'm sorry; I wish I could be smoother; I'll never be able to do this; you'll never want to dance with me again!" and other similar sentiments.

Finally, Robert just looked at me and said, "Quit whining!" He was laughing when he said it, but it really hit home with me. Here I am, a motivational speaker who prides herself on having a tremendously positive attitude, and I'm whining! I made a pact with myself right then to approach things differently. I told Robert he could step on my foot if he thought I was whining again, and we made a deal that every time I said "I'm sorry" it would cost me a dollar! Believe me, I learned to articulate my concerns in much more positive and constructive ways — and I had a much better attitude about myself as a dancer!

5 KEYS TO ENRICHING RELATIONSHIPS

- Do something for another person without anyone knowing about it.

- Never let the sun set on your anger. Take initiative to resolve the issue.

- Tell someone you love them . . . and then act as if it were true.

- Support other people's dreams and goals.

- Resist the temptation to give advice. Instead, give smiles.

No pessimist ever discovered the secrets of the stars, or sailed to an unchartered land, or opened a new heaven to the human spirit.

(Helen Keller)

LOOK FOR THE JOY IN THE COMPETITION

Relationships can take a real beating in the midst of competition. It becomes easy to focus on the result of the event, rather than remember that the joy is in the activity. This came home to me several years ago, as I was watching an NBA playoff game on T.V.

We are Michael Jordan fans, and were enjoying the final game in the playoff series between the Chicago Bulls and the New York Knicks. The score was very close, and time was running out. This was a "Do or Die" game for both teams, and it was anyone's game. Suddenly there was a loose ball, and several players from both teams were scrambling on the floor, fighting for possession. Finally, the referee blew his whistle.

I'll never forget the picture on the screen at that instant. It was classic! Michael Jordan and a Knicks player (sorry, I don't remember who — remember, I'm a Jordan fan!) were both grabbing the ball. At the sound of the whistle, they both froze, then looked at each other and smiled. I mean, they really grinned at each other. You could almost hear them saying, "Wow! Isn't this FUN?"

Even in the midst of tremendous pressure, both these players were able to enjoy the moment, and feel the joy of the activity they had trained so diligently for. What a powerful lesson for each of us. Let's be sure, in the midst of pressures and competition, to enjoy the moment. That's what it's all about.

THE POWER OF TOUCH

When bank tellers place change in the hand of the customer rather than on the counter, the customer's perceptions of the bank rise sharply.

Servers in restaurants who touched customers when giving change or a receipt found tips increased dramatically.

AFTERGLOW SESSIONS: Pacific Lutheran Football Coach Frosty Westering is the winningest active coach in NAIA football with 236 wins. His methods are somewhat unorthodox, but can teach us all a lesson in human relations. He starts the season with three days of team building. There's no swearing; no trash talk; players hold hands running on and off the field; fumbles and interceptions are punished with hugs instead of a bawling out.

In 'afterglow sessions' after each game, talk is limited to big plays and standout performances. Since becoming coach in 1972, Westering has affirmed, complimented, encouraged and praised his teams to three NAIA Division II championships. He's never had a losing season.

"We believe the best thing is to affirm and encourage our players, even when they make mistakes," says Westering. "If they aren't down on themselves, the next hit, the next pass could make the difference."

(USA Today, 09/12/95)

Understand that your parents, teachers and friends did the best they could, considering their past programming, needs, pressures, and hang-ups. What they didn't give you, they didn't have to give.

(Jane Boucher)

WHEN TEMPTED TO GOSSIP

Gossip is one of the most destructive forces in relationships. Here's my philosophy when tempted to say something that could be potentially harmful or negative about another person: If you wouldn't put it in writing, sign it and post it where everyone could see it — *don't say it!*

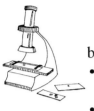

IF NEEDS BE

A vast body of research suggests that there are three basic categories of interpersonal needs:

- *Inclusion* — The need to include others in our various activities and to be included in the activities of others.
- *Control* — The need for some sort of control over other people and situations, and the need to be influenced by others.
- *Affection* — The need to give and receive caring and affection . . . to be liked.

As you look at your lifestyle, which of these needs seems to be most prominent? Not everyone needs or wants to belong to a lot of organizations; not everyone needs to be 'liked'; not everyone enjoys the feeling of power. By recognizing what it is you need to give — and need to receive from others, you become better able to balance your activities to meet your needs. Understanding this principle also helps you relate to others more appropriately. Make it okay for people to be who they are.

HOME ALONE

Learn to be comfortable being with yourself. I find that I sometimes *need* to be alone. What's interesting is I'm discovering that my time alone helps me clarify what I want or need from others. My hibernations seem to ground me. I feel more settled … more tolerant … less encumbered. When it is time to put on my public face and join others again, I can do so with enthusiasm, purpose and composure. What I'm saying is that, for me, brief periods of aloneness help the *social me* value my friendships and colleagueships all the more … The contrast is simple … more straight-forward and rewarding.

Gee, it's nice to be alone . . . sometimes.

(Rod McKuen)

SMALL TALK

People criticize small talk, and consider it a waste of time. But small talk serves a critical function in relationship development. Through small talk, we learn little things about the other person that become entry points to a deeper relationship. Small talk helps us recognize whether or not we want to move on to 'big' talk by deepening the relationship. I firmly believe that many relationships would be improved if the individuals involved would engage in periodic small talk, to rediscover the joy of who they are and what they mean to each other.

Small is BIG — so look for ways to do small things for people that say "I care. You matter." You'll be amazed at how big their appreciation is!

THE JOY OF SMALL GIFTS

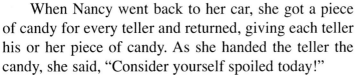

My Program Administrator, Nancy, told me of a ritual she has. When she goes through the drive-through window at her bank, she always send a piece of candy with her transaction to the teller. One day, she had several transactions to handle and so, she went inside. The tellers behind the counter told Nancy how "spoiled" the drive-through teller was by getting candy.

When Nancy went back to her car, she got a piece of candy for every teller and returned, giving each teller his or her piece of candy. As she handed the teller the candy, she said, "Consider yourself spoiled today!"

The tellers are still talking about it, and Nancy said it was so much fun to do a small thing for a person — they are so appreciative!

DON'T WAIT TO SHOW SOMEONE
YOU CARE

An extremely powerful example of a nurturing relationship is seen in Christopher and Dana Reeve. When Christopher Reeve was paralyzed from neck down as a result of being thrown from his horse, he claims it was his wife, Dana's words that kept him alive. She said, quite simply, "It's you I love. And I'll be here for you, no matter what."

On an interview, she hugged Chris after he said something, and it struck me then that he was not able to hug her back. He could only show her his love through his eyes and his voice.

Never take for granted your ability to hug someone you love, or play with your children, or walk with your pet, or work in your community. Don't wait to show someone how important they are to you.

> On March 1,1998, at a special event honoring Christopher Reeve, and to raise awareness and money for spinal injury research, Stevie Wonder said these words: "Just because a man cannot see doesn't mean he has no vision; just because a man cannot walk doesn't mean he cannot go the distance."

I don't know what your destiny will be, but one thing I do know: the only ones among you who will be really happy are those who have sought and found how to serve.

(Albert Schweitzer)

TAKE A COFFEE BREAK

Make time to have coffee with someone you do not know very well. The brief time spent together, sharing trivial information about each other, can break down barriers and build bridges to new friendships.

UNCONTROLLED ANGER — Today's high paced, high stress lifestyle has created frayed nerves and uncontrollable anger in people. You never know how someone will react to something you do. We are seeing a dramatic increase in violence in what would normally be fairly normal situations.

A case in point occurred at the New York International Auto Show. A young man was photographing the new model at the BMW exhibit, when another man accidentally stepped in front of him. The man with the camera pulled a knife and stabbed the other man, who in turn pulled out his own knife and stabbed the man with the camera.

(NY Times, 4/13/98)

PLAY THE PART

In one of my college drama classes, I had to perform a scene demonstrating emotion. A fellow student and I selected a great scene,which required us to scream at each other — I even got to throw things! Do you think, when we got off stage, we were angry with each other for the nasty things we said? Of course not. We knew we were just "playing a part."

The next time you have to deal with a nasty or irritable person, just tell yourself that they are playing the part

of an obnoxious jerk (and doing a fabulous job of it —
academy award winning material!). You are going to play
the part of someone who can handle that type of person
with ease and confidence. This helps you take one step
away from the situation, and handle it nondefensively. It is
amazing how effective this technique can be.

BEST OF THE YEAR!

Create a "Best Accomplishments of the Year"
Calendar for work, family or volunteer organization.
Include everyone's picture, name and outstanding achieve-
ment(s). Let everyone participate by submitting their own
ideas of the "best of the best" things that have occurred
during the year.

PUBLIC THANK YOUS

If you were able to publicly thank everyone who has
helped you achieve success, who would you include in the
list? Why? Who are the top two or three people who have
helped you the most? What made their contributions so
special? Have you told them lately how much they helped
you? In what ways have you helped them? Have you spon-
sored anyone else's success?

I WAS GLAD I WROTE

One day several years ago, I opened my mail to find
an announcement from my alma mater, sharing the news
that the Dean of Student Affairs, Sam Ross, had been promoted to the role of Assistant to the President. The letter
took me back to my college days, and I remembered how
Dr. Ross has done so much to help me with financial aid
and getting a job on campus. On the spur of the moment, I
followed my intuition and wrote him a congratulatory
note. I mentioned that he probably did not remember me,
but I certainly remembered him, and all his help in making

it financially possible for me to attend the college. I explained how valuable my college degree had been, and what I was doing now. It was a brief note . . . nothing major.

Less than two weeks later, I got a reply. Dr. Ross thanked me for taking time to write. "So few students ever let us know that what we do matters," he wrote. "It's nice to know someone remembers."

Not too many months later, I received another correspondence from the college. This time, it was a sad announcement that Dr. Ross, while on vacation with his family, had died suddenly of a heart attack.

As I stood there, holding that announcement, chills ran through my body. In fact, as I am typing this story, the chills have returned. I keep thinking, "What if I'd waited to write to him?" I'm so glad I followed my intuition, and let him know that what he did for me was appreciated — before it was too late.

LOVE LETTER FROM HEAVEN

Imagine waiting anxiously for your 16-year-old son to get home from school so you could give him a big hug. You had just received a letter from him in the mail, written as a school assignment. The letter thanked his parents for making his childhood so good, and for all they had given him. It ended with the words: 'I love you both. Lovingly Yours, Michael'.

Instead of giving her son that hug, his mother answered her door to a State Highway Patrol Trooper who told her that Michael had been killed as a passenger in a single-vehicle wreck on his way home from school. His mother feels that his letter was a godsend. It helped give her a feeling of closure, along with the knowledge of his love.

Take time to say 'I love you' and "what you do matters to me.' You never know when it may be the last time you'll get the opportunity to say those words . . . and you never know what it will mean to the other person. (*Raleigh N&O*, December 14, 1997)

TIP FOR A LONG, HAPPY RELATIONSHIP

A woman who was celebrating her 50th wedding anniversary shared a wonderful piece of advice to her younger friends who were asking how they, too, could experience a long, happy relationship. She said that when she found she was serious about the man who eventually was to become her husband, she decided to make a list of his ten biggest faults which, for the sake of a happy and lasting relationship, she was willing to overlook and accept. When folks begged her to share what some of the faults she had listed were, she chuckled wisely and said, "To tell you the truth, I never really made that list. But whenever my husband did something that made me really angry, I would say to myself 'Lucky for him that's one of the ten!'

ALWAYS LEAVE 'EM AN OUT

When you are giving constructive criticism to another person, always leave them a way to gracefully retreat. For example, instead of saying "You know I'm allergic to cigarette smoke. Quit smoking around me," you might try saying "Perhaps you're not aware that I'm allergic to cigarette smoke. I'd sure appreciate it if you would go somewhere else to finish your cigarette. Then we can finish our discussion."

Another example: Instead of blaming a problem on the other person, simply say "Evidently we had a communication problem." or "I guess I wasn't as clear in my directions as I thought . . ."

Remember, the goal is to clear up a problem, not back a person into a corner. By leaving them an "out," you make it possible for them to swing over to your way of thinking quite easily.

TRY RED SKELTON'S TECHNIQUE

Red Skelton, the world-renowned clown best know for his Clem Kadiddlehopper and Freddie Freeloader characters, had an interesting technique for dealing with people who hurt him. He explained it in the New York Times this way: "When anyone hurts us, my wife and I sit in our Japanese sand garden and drink iced tea. There are five stones in the garden — for sky, wind, fire, water and earth. We sit and think of five of the nicest things we can about the person who hurt us. If he hurts us a second time, we do the same thing. The third time, we light a candle and he is, for us, dead.·

LEARN FROM YOUR COMPETITION

When tennis great Chris Everett retired from professional competition, her strongest opponent, Martina Navatralova, asked her the following question: "When you beat me, how did you do it?" She learned from Chris's feedback that she had a weak backhand. She worked to improve it, and became an even stronger champion than before.

BEWARE OF 'CHECKOUT RAGE': In
Milwaukee, Wisconsin a supermarket customer was charged with cutting off part of the nose of a woman who went to an express checkout lane with too many items. The victim was slashed with a pocket knife in a parking lot, lost about half her nose and had to undergo surgery. A clerk whose express lane was empty motioned the woman through with more than 10 items. Next time that happens to you, think twice before you comply!

(*N&O*, Raleigh, NC 04/12/98)

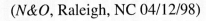

LET THE OTHER PERSON BE RIGHT

Sometimes it just isn't worth a fight. Before you come back with a statement you know will lead to another round, ask yourself: Is this worth an argument? If the answer is "NO," then don't say it! Even if you know, deep down, that you're right and they're wrong, if it doesn't really matter, let it go!

I remember two friends of mine who had attended a convention. They were telling me about it, and one said, "The best speaker was Wednesday afternoon. He was great! He talked about creative marketing techniques . . . "

The other friend interrupted: "No, no, no. He was on Tuesday afternoon."

"I'm sure it was Wednesday," exclaimed friend number 1. "I distinctly remember . . . "

"No, it was Tuesday, because I'd just come back from my meeting."

They argued about whether it was Tuesday or Wednesday until they left to get the conference brochure to determine who was right. I'm standing there thinking, "Who cares? Does it matter?" I just wanted to know about the creative marketing techniques.

Don't hold grudges. While you're holding grudges, they're out dancing!"

(Buddy Hackett)

THE PERFECT "OTHER"

Select some relationship that needs work. It could be your relationship with your spouse or 'significant other', your boss, your child, a parent, a coworker, a neighbor, an employee of yours, etc.

At the top of a sheet of paper, write the words "The Perfect _____." Fill in the appropriate word to describe the other person in the relationship you selected (The Perfect Husband; Boss; Son; etc.)

Make a list of no less than 25 specific characteristics that would describe that "perfect other."

That was the fun part! Now comes the hard work. Flip the paper over, and write these words: In order to deserve that perfect _____, I need to be . . .

You guessed it! It's time to make a list of no less than 25 specific characteristics describing how you need to be, in order to deserve that perfect other. Then focus on this list, and begin working on your behaviors. You'll be amazed at the impact your changes have on the behaviors of those around you.

HOW TO HANDLE A 'NAYSAYER'

Do you ever find yourself face-to-face with a person who constantly uses the phrase "That won't work because . . ." They are generally critical of every idea that comes down the pike, and are quick to deflate any excitement you have about something new or challenging.

When you meet up with one of these naysayers, improve your relationship with them by sanctioning their role of Devil's Advocate. When you share a new idea or concept with them, follow up with the statement: "Now, why don't you be my Devil's Advocate, and help me think about what could go wrong? What have I overlooked? What are possible roadblocks?"

THE 4 R'S TO DEAL WITH GOSSIPERS

Gossipers love to talk about other people, with a focus on their negative points or problems. Not only are they annoying to be around, they can be destructive to people's reputations as well. Use one or more techniques from this 4-R Formula to help you eliminate gossipers from your life.

Refuse to participate. Do not add fuel to the fire by showing interest in what the gossiper is saying, or by adding any tidbits you may have heard from others.

Request verification. If it is appropriate, ask the gossiper for facts to support the information. By saying, "Let's go ask him if that's true," you shut the gossiper right up! You are no fun to talk with at all!

Refocus the conversation. Change topics and focus on something else.

Relocate yourself! Simply say "I'm not interested" and walk away.

 If dogs could talk, I wonder if they would still be 'man's best friend'?

ELEANOR ROOSEVELT'S ADVICE

 For years, I kept a quote by Eleanor Roosevelt on my desk, to remind me not to be intimidated by other people. She said: "No one can make you feel inferior without your consent." You can actually insert any word where it says inferior. No one can make you feel anything (angry, dumb, ugly, fat, silly, intimidated, or any other thing) unless you give them permission. Don't give away your power by allowing the words of others to affect you. Just because they said it doesn't make it true!

One of my workshop participants paraphrased her quote this way: "No one can get your goat if they don't know where you tie it."

THE 'JESSICA FLETCHER TECHNIQUE' FOR KNOW-IT-ALLS

 I call this the Jessica Fletcher Technique, because it was so well demonstrated on the popular television show Murder, She Wrote. Jessica Fletcher was an author of murder mysteries, who somehow managed to find herself embroiled in a murder everywhere she went. Of course, she was the person who always solved the case.

Jessica was a master in dealing with Know-It-Alls, particularly those from the police force. When faced with a defensive sheriff with an inflated ego, Jessica had a way of getting what she wanted by making them think it was their idea. For example, she would say to the officer, "I'm sure you don't want anyone to leave until you've taken their finger prints" or "I'm sure you noticed the carnation lying on the floor by the body."

Naturally, the egotistical police officer would jump on her suggestion, and make it his or her own. That's the secret when dealing with people who use their credentials, age, service time, professional status, etc. to prove their knowledge and wisdom. These people want center stage, and will get defensive when challenged. So use their ego against them by giving them the ideas you want them to have.

By the way, sucking up never hurts either! Acknowledge their status, and let them know you value the expertise they bring to the situation.

The longing for interpersonal intimacy stays with every human being from infancy throughout life; and there is no human being who is not threatened by its loss.
(Frieda Fromm-Reichmann)

FORGIVE AND FORGET? NOT!

It's unrealistic to think you can actually forget something, even though you do forgive. A better principle — and more achievable — is to forgive and release. Release the anger, hurt, pain and other negative emotions, and focus on healing.

FAMILY TIES

Here are a few simple strategies to help strengthen family relationships:

- Try not to behave "like family." Try to treat family more like friends.
- Do a reality check. Don't expect the perfect get together. We set too high of expectations, then are disappointed. Be realistic — this isn't a television show where everyone has a script to follow!
- Plan ahead for emotional pitfalls. Think and talk about what might bother other family members (inappropriate television shows; cutesy nicknames; etc.) and agree as a family how to handle problems that arise.
- Don't insist that everyone take part in everything. Give everyone opportunities to do things they enjoy, at their pace, on their own.
- Postpone conflicts. A social occasion is not the time to debate who will get the family silver, or criticize your son for quitting his job.
- Release the past. Okay, so mom did like your brother best! What's the point of focusing on it twenty years later? Everyone makes mistakes. Forgive them, and move on with your life. (Adapted from Parade Magazine, March 15, 1998)

SPIRITUAL DEVOTION

Dr. Laura Schlessinger talks about the need for spiritual devotion in our lives. She says, "It helps us temper our perceived sense of importance with our true importance, which can be realized only by devoting time, attention, care and devotion to others. Without such devotion, our lives lose meaning. Without meaning, we lose purpose. Without purpose, we lose ourselves.

It is neither serious, nor sincere, to apologize but not to back up the apology with action where action is appropriate.

(Marianne Williamson, The Healing of America)

I do not have to react to criticism with hurt feelings. It is my interpretation of the meaning for me that produces the pain. I believe that if I were more fully conscious and acceptant of the way I am, if I were more familiar with "me," I would not feel so criticized or complimented by people's words but would be confident to judge their accuracy for myself.

(Hugh Prather)

RELEASE YOUR GRUDGES

You've heard the old saying, 'Forgive and forget' — and probably also heard people say, "I can forgive, but I'll never forget!" Hanging on to anger, grudges, hurt, or any other negative feelings you have toward another person doesn't hurt them at all! But it sure takes its emotional toll on you. A grudge is any unresolved anger we hold inside; it feeds on itself and festers and grows. Research has demonstrated that consistent grudges can lead to stress, backaches, chest pains, migraine headaches, relationship and even job-related problems. It creates low self-esteem within the grudge-bearer, and can even manifest itself in negative psychological traits. The message — loud and clear — is, holding a grudge hurts you, not the person you're holding the grudge against!

I acknowledge that forgetting may be a little unrealistic, but we can certainly forgive and release any ill will we are harboring against another. In other words, practice the Law of Forgiveness.

There is an old saying that a donkey may carry a heavy load of precious cargo on its back without knowing the cargo's value — feeling only the weight of circumstances and never fully appreciating its worth. We often carry so much psychological baggage around with us that it crushes our creative potential. Begin now to release past grudges and free yourself for prosperity and joy.

GUIDED MEDITATION FOR FORGIVENESS

This beautiful guided meditation, created by Bil Holton, can assist you in the difficult task of releasing grudges, and forgiving. I recommend that you (or someone with a calm, clear voice) read the meditation onto a tape. Find a comfortable place where you will not be disturbed for about ten minutes. Get relaxed, take several deep breaths — slowly — then let the tape play while you close your eyes and flow through this process.

§ § § § § § § § §

In your mind's eye, see yourself in your favorite place. This special place can be out-of-doors or indoors. You might see yourself standing near a stream or a large mountain lake, or maybe even on a tropical beach. You could find yourself in a sauna or steamroom or visiting a museum or art gallery. Wherever that special place is, take a moment to examine every detail. What colors do you see? Are there any special sounds or odors? Any unusual textures or shapes?

As you fully relax and enjoy your Shangri La, know that you are safe and secure in the arms of the Universe. This is your place. A place of quiet and peace. Joy. Serenity. Forgiveness. It is a place where the forgiving heart embraces others with a feeling of compassion for whatever stage they are experiencing in their soul's evolu-

tion ... A place filled with feelings of love and oneness rather than judgment.

The forgiving heart knows that when it feels separate from those less evolved, it also separates itself from those who are more evolved, thus delaying its own journey upward.

If you have a past experience which caused pain or discomfort — one which you find difficult to release — begin to see in your mind's eye the person or people involved. These people may be alive, or perhaps they have made their transition. It doesn't matter, because this special place knows no time limits.

The hurt may have been caused yesterday, last year, or a lifetime ago. You did not deserve the hurt. It went deep — deep enough to lodge itself in your memory. And it keeps hurting you now. It's one of those old pains that doesn't heal so easily. It remains like a stubborn stain in the fabric of your memory. Perhaps a friend betrayed you; someone special lied to you; a stranger hurt you; a parent neglected or abused you; a brother or sister angered you; a spouse was unfaithful; a co-worker cheated you ...

It is not necessary to replay the event or circumstance which upset you. If your old script has started, gently end it by seeing yourself standing in your favorite place. You feel peaceful and relaxed. You are aware that you are safe and secure in the arms of the Universe. This special place is your sanctuary. You are filled with love and understanding for all things.

You know it is in this quiet place that your hurts and pains are dissolved and released — never to resurrect or impede your happiness again. You are happy and want to rid yourself of an old self-defeating script that has been replayed for much too long now. So, at this time invite that person who you believe has caused you so much anguish into your sanctuary.

As this person approaches — simply smile and say, "I forgive you and release you for any harm I believe you have caused me." As this person faces you, you realize that this, too, is a child of God, one who is trying to find self-hood and peace, happiness and joy — just like you.

You may even discover that YOU are this other person. Too often, we forget or find it difficult to forgive ourselves, and self-forgiveness is perfectly okay — even vital. So whether it is another person or yourself you are facing, simply reach out and shake hands — or hold that dear, wonderful human being in an embrace of friendship. And as the two of you make peace, know that the healing process has begun. Then if there is someone else who needs your forgiveness, invite that person into your special sanctuary, too. Release any ill feelings, guilt or animosity and greet that person with love in your heart. Release them to their highest good, knowing that your relationship with them is now loving and filled with new-found understanding.

When you forgive someone for hurting you, you perform spiritual surgery on your soul. If you cannot free yourself or others from wrongs you feel have been inflicted on you or release them to their own greatest good, you enslave yourself to your painful past. Forgiveness opens your heart to your own good. You will know that forgiveness has begun when you feel the power to wish transgressors well. We make new beginnings, not where we used to be — or wish we could be — but where we are in this now moment.

Know that there is no need to feel regret or guilt about the past. You have just repaired the damage — you have just healed the hurt — you have just cleared the log jam that placed your health and happiness in jeopardy. You are free. A tremendous weight has been lifted. You are free! You are free!

As you prepare to leave your special place, know that you can visit it as often as you like. Know that you have released the ties that bound you to the past. You have taken a quantum leap toward self-fulfillment and happiness.

Slowly become aware of the sounds and sensations surrounding you. Whenever you are ready, you may open your eyes and return to the real world, knowing you are now a different person, having released the weight of your negative feelings. You are free, and receptive to the prosperity which is coming to you.

§ § § § § § § § § §

Welcome back! If you truly experienced this activity, you feel lighter . . . free-er . . . and perhaps somewhat emotional. It's Okay. Just know that you will never be the same again. The greatest step you can take toward your own evolvement and inner peace is to release any grudges, blame or hard feelings you're hanging on to. Forgiveness is a quantum leap toward inner peace!

When you forgive and release, you attract a burst of energy, radiant joy and inner peace.

THE TOP FIVE DYNAMITE STRATEGIES TO BUILD YOUR CREDIBILITY

People do not like to interact with people they cannot trust — period. One of the most critical areas to develop, in order to enrich your interpersonal relationships, is your credibility. Credibility and trust cannot be mandated; they must be earned. Here are 5 Dynamite Strategies to help you.

Be Correct. Very few people give wrong information on purpose. The problem is, they give quick responses without considering all the information, or they just base their response or assumptions of misunderstandings. When someone asks you a question, be sure you take it seriously enough to clarify exactly what they want to know, and how the information will be used.

Be Clear. Unfortunately, it seems that when we know something really well, we are at our worst in explaining it to others. We use jargon, omit information that is obvious to us, or get so bogged down in detail that our listener's eyes glaze over. When giving information, take responsibility to be sure you were understood. It will avoid misunderstandings down the road.

Avoid Exaggeration. We often resort to exaggeration to make our point, or to avoid an unrealistic expectation, or to make ourselves look better. But exaggeration leads to a decrease in our credibility. Be honest — even if it hurts.

Keep Confidences. One of the fastest ways to break a trust is to share something that was told to you in confidence. If you find yourself saying, "I really shouldn't be telling you this . . .," then don't.

Do What You Say You're Going To Do. This is really the bottom line in trust and credibility. If you say you're going to complete something by a certain date, do it. If you find you are unable to meet a commitment, inform the affected people as quickly as possible. People can handle information better than surprises!

Don't make promises until you thoroughly understand what you have to do, what impact the promise will have on your other commitments, and the importance of the promise to your own goals.
                                   (Paula Peisner)

PREDICTIONS FOR THE FUTURE

Futurists predict that computer generated friendship circles will identify people around the world with whom you may share common interests. New tribes of kindred spirits will unite parents who homeschool, gardeners who practice organic farming, upwardly mobile professionals who bowl, etc. This will allow marketers to target these groups with products and pitches designed especially for them.

"Packaged" holidays and other celebrations will help reduce stress for busy families by having entrepreneurs come in and decorate the home, deliver packaged meals, and even purchase and wrap gifts.

Libraries will become virtual, condensing their book sections to make room for computer labs. Futuristic fabrics will allow the ultimate personalization of your wardrobe. For example, there will be massaging fabrics for relieving stress, fabrics that emit favorite scents and aromatherapies, and even clothing with cooling and heating systems, periodic self-cleaning and self-repair. And how about a navigational jacket that enables us to locate anyone any place?

With all the high tech innovations, it is interesting that one prediction is that simple pleasures from times past, such as sewing and quilting bees, will emerge as an antidote to today's chaotic lifestyles. Also, comfort foods served on everyday china will replace sophisticated gourmet meals on most consumer's menus.

(Futurist, June-July, 1998)

We need old friends to help us grow old, and new friends
to help us stay young.

(Letty Cottin Pogrebin)

Ralph Waldo Emerson, in his wisdom wrote: *It is easy in the world to live after the world's opinion; it is easy in solitude to live after our own; but the great person is the one who in the midst of the crowd keeps with perfect sweetness the independence of solitude.*

A NETWORK OF REDWOODS

Have you ever had the opportunity of visiting a magnificent redwood forest? These trees are gigantic! They punch holes in the sky two hundred — even three hundred feet high. One particularly large tree has a hole cut in its trunk large enough for cars to drive through! As I was wandering through this wonderful forest, I commented that the root system for redwood trees must be very deep, since the trees were so tall. A guide nearby heard my remark and quickly corrected me. He informed us that the redwood trees get their nourishment from the surface moisture. Their root systems are actually very shallow.

My next question was: How on earth do these trees maintain their stability? Simple. They don't stand alone. Their root systems interlock and intertwine into a vast patchwork quilt of tentacled roots. When the winds and storms come, those incredible redwoods stand solid, because they support and sustain one another.

What a developmental lesson we can learn from the redwoods. We need to "spread out our roots" and interlock and intertwine with other people, so that when the storms of life hit us, we know we have others who will support and sustain us.

BUILDING YOUR NETWORK

What does your current "network of redwoods" look like? It is important to make the effort to build the network appropriate for you. When the storms hit, it's too late to start the process. It must already be in place. Assess your current support system, and make sure it includes:

- Close Friends who love and support you in spite of your fallacies;
- Energizers who motivate you when the going gets tough;
- Experts who provide information and expertise in your field of interest;
- Challengers who force you to stretch yourself to new heights;
- Mentors who already are where you want to go professionally;
- Access Providers who help you cut through red tape and gain access to the resources you need.

Developing your Network of Redwoods is not a one-shot deal. It is a constantly evolving process. You'll find people moving in and out of your network as your needs (and theirs) change. I urge you to do regular maintenance checks on your network to keep the relationships alive, active, relevant and healthy.

Remember the cardinal rule of networking: what you send out will come back multiplied. You must actively help and support others if you expect help and support in return. Reciprocate. Accommodate. Motivate. Challenge. Remember the folks in your network with thoughtful notes, phone calls, and visits when you *don't* need their help. This type of "regular feeding" will keep your forest growing.

The ability to resign, to let go of obsolete responses, of *exhausted relationships and of tasks beyond one's potential is an essential part of the wisdom of living.*

(Frederick Perls)

NEVER, NEVER, NEVER . . .

Value each precious moment you have with a person you love. Never miss an opportunity to say "I love you." Never let the sun set on your anger. Never take for granted the special closeness you share. Never go through a day without having fun. Never forget to express what you like about them. Never lose an opportunity to cherish them.

The most wonderful of all things in life, I believe, is the discovery of another human being with whom one's relationship has a glowing depth, beauty, and joy as the years increase.

(Sir Hugh Walpole)

Live with the knowledge that the best is always yet to come!

TRANSFORMING
TIME ROBBERS

TRANSFORMING TIME ROBBERS—
SNEAK PEEK

Imagine that a new bank has just moved into your area. They have notified you of a new account that has been opened in your name. It is very unique. Every morning, bright and early, a deposit of $86,400 is made into your account. The only catch is this: at the end of the day, any money left in your account will be removed, and it is gone forever. But next morning, another $86,400 gets deposited.

What do you think you would do each day? Naturally, you would make sure that money was removed so none of it went back to the bank! You'd pay bills, go shopping (big time!), give some to friends and loved ones, invest some, blow some! No matter what, you wouldn't leave it in the bank to waste away.

The good news is that you have this account. But before you quit your job, let me clarify! It's not money, but time. Every morning you get 86,400 seconds given to you. And at day's end, they are gone forever. Horace Mann said it so well: "Lost, yesterday, somewhere between sunrise and sunset, two golden hours, each set with 60 diamond minutes. No reward is offered, for they are gone forever." We don't let other people spend our money — so why do we let them spend our time?

Time: It is the one thing everyone complains they don't have enough of — and yet each of us has all there is. Time truly is an "Equal Opportunity Employer." Every person, regardless of their status or background . . . regardless of how much money they earn . . . regardless of who they know . . . receives 24 hours per day, divided into 60-minute segments. No one has more — no one has less. But some people still manage to accomplish so much more from their time allotment than others.

What is the secret? How can we squeeze every possible use out of every minute we are granted? This section is packed with practical principles, tools and motivators designed to help you understand the concept of time as a resource, attack your personal time robbers, and get the most out of every day you have the privilege of living on this planet!

THE WORK/HOME TRIGGER POINT

It is a real challenge to focus on work when you're at work, and on home when you're at home. Too often we carry our work home with us, both physically and mentally, or we end up at the office with our mind still on issues from our personal life. Here's a technique to help you gain that sense of focus you need to "be present" where you are.

Evaluate the travel route you take to work, and identify the half-way point in your journey. Find some concrete, permanent item that marks that half-way point. It might be a gas station, a house, a billboard, a unique tree, etc. Make it something very obvious that is easily seen as you make your commute. This item is your "Trigger Point."

As you leave your house for work, it is fine to be thinking about what is happening at home. You can have it on your mind until you reach your "Trigger Point." At the moment you see the "Trigger Point," force yourself to shift your thinking to where you are going. Begin to plan your work day; recap in your mind the key issues to cover in an upcoming meeting; mentally review your calendar; think about your work area and the people you will be interacting with. If your mind wanders back to issues from home, simply acknowledge them, then force your thoughts back to work. By the time you arrive, your mind should be cleared and focused on the work you are there to perform.

When you leave work, you will be doing the same thing in reverse. As you leave, you will — quite naturally — be thinking about the job. You may be reliving a rough experience, regretting some unfinished project, rejoicing over a victory, or planning for the next day. Go ahead and think about work all you want until you see your "Trigger Point." At that moment, begin forcing yourself to think about where you are going instead of where you've been. Think about your home, what you are going to be doing, who you will be seeing, etc. As before, if your mind wanders back to issues from work, simply acknowledge them, then force your thoughts back to home. By the time you arrive, your mind should be cleared and focused on the people and activities you are about to become involved with.

THE GARAGE DOOR TIME CLOCK

This illustration came from Roger, a participant in one of my stress management workshops. After I had shared the Work/Home Trigger Point technique, Roger excitedly shared something he does to focus him when he comes home from work. He has an electric garage door opener in his car, and when he pulls up and clicks the button to raise the door, he says to himself that he is now clocking in on his other (most important) job — husband and father. As soon as he hears that click, he considers himself 'on the clock' with this job, and leaves the other job behind, to pick up when he leaves the next morning.

JIM CROCE'S LESSON

In the early 1970's, the singer Jim Croce wrote a beautiful song entitled *Time in a Bottle*. The chorus states: "There never seems to be enough time to do the things you want to do, once you find them . . . " In September of 1973, soon after this song came out, Jim Croce was killed in a tragic plane crash. It's almost as if he had some intuitive vision of his destiny as he penned those words.

I don't like to scare people by telling them we never know how much time we have, but folks . . . we never know how much time we have! And there truly never is enough time to do the things you want to do. There's not even enough time to do the important things you want to do. That's why it's so critical to be very picky about how you choose to spend the time you have. Choose carefully how you spend your seconds, for your seconds become your minutes, your minutes become your hours, your hours become your days, your days become your weeks, and your weeks become your years. Your years become your life, and there are no sadder words on earth than looking back over your life and saying "I wish I had . . ."

THE MAGIC SIGN FOR PROCRASTINATORS

If you find you are procrastinating often, try this simple, but effective strategy. On a 3x5" card, in great big letters, write these words: DO IT NOW!

Stick the card on your wall, or tape it on your desk or counter top. This is so strange, but I promise it's true. You'll forget all about the sign. You won't even see it — until you procrastinate. All of a sudden, it will seem as if it lights up like a neon sign, blinking on and off — reminding you that you are procrastinating!

You will do one of two things. You'll either feel so guilty that you'll take action and do whatever it is you are procrastinating on — or — in disgust, you'll rip the sign off the wall or counter top, tear it into tiny pieces and throw it in the trash can, hating the day you ever learned this technique. But if you chose the second option, a very strange phenomenon occurs. The sign gets a voice. You actually hear it coming up from the trash

can, saying "Do it now! Do it now!" You can't avoid it!
You might as well take action, and do it . . . NOW!

*Understanding how your daily efforts contribute to
accomplishing what you value makes your work meaningful and satisfying. Do something toward your lifetime
accomplishments and lifestyle every day. You'll feel great.*
(Dru Scott)

KEEP ONLY ONE CALENDAR

Forget about juggling all the calendars from your
life. Consolidate everything (personal and professional)
into one, including scheduled meetings, entertainment
dates, birthdays and anniversaries, memory joggers to
yourself, etc. Consider using the simplest method possible. Look at it each night, to remind yourself of the next
day's schedule.

START A TICKLER FILE

Place 12 file folders in a box, labeled for each month.
In front of these, place 31 file sheets, labeled 1 through 31,
which represent each day of the current month. Anything
needing to be done in this current month (i.e., bills to be
paid, cards sent, issues followed up on, responses to letters,
reminders of appointments, etc.) is placed behind the number representing the day you want to do that particular
thing.

For instance, if you pay your bills on the 15th, place
all statements you receive behind the file sheet labeled 15.
If you want to mail your brother a birthday card on the
22nd, place the card you bought and addressed behind the
file sheet labeled 22. Each day, look behind the day's tickler sheet to discover things you need to do that day. Then
move that file sheet to the back of the numbered sheets, so
the first sheet facing you is always the next day's. (If it's

not, it means you forgot to check your tickler file — and something may be waiting to be done!)

Anything with a "Do Date" other than the current month simply gets thrown into the appropriate monthly file. At the end of each month, open the next month's file and distribute the contents behind the appropriate days.

Once you start using this tool, you will wonder how you ever functioned without it.

A MONTHLY CARD SHOP

Purchase all the greeting cards you anticipate needing for the month at one time. Go ahead and address the cards, and tickle the date each should be sent (See Tickler File technique). Don't seal them — you might want to add a brief note the day you send the card.

Time is life. It is irreversible and irreplaceable. To waste your time is to waste your life, but to master your time is to master your life and make the most of it.

(Alan Lakein)

THE DOT TEST

One of the biggest sources of frustration is that stack of papers on your desk. It has been estimated that the average person wastes 7 hours a week just shuffling paper around, looking through piles, or searching the in-box. Discover if you're guilty. For just two weeks, try this test. Every time you touch a piece of paper, for whatever reason, make a little red dot at the top. Here's the kicker: when you pick up a piece of paper and notice it has something like 37 dots at the top, guess what? You're guilty of just moving it around! You've confused activity with accomplishment. It's time to do something with that paper (see the R.A.F.T. Technique on page 255).

Bring some harmony to your life by applying this Harmony Principle: Every time you touch a piece of paper, move it one step closer to completion — or — throw it away!!

Too Busy? In Tinley Park, Illinois, a mother accidentally left her two month old son, strapped in his car seat, on top of her car. He fell off when the woman drove away, tumbling face-down in a busy intersection. The infant suffered some cuts and scrapes but was not severely injured . . . The mother had traveled about two blocks when the baby slid off; she then drove another five miles before realizing what had happened.   (*N&O*, Raleigh, NC, 12/22/97)

When your daily activities are in concert with your highest priorities, then you'll have inner peace.

(Hiram Smith)

THE TEN-MINUTE JUMP START

Are you a procrastinator? Please do not put off this technique until tomorrow! Although everyone procrastinates, some people make a living out of delay tactics. The Ten-Minute Jump Start Technique is one of the best techniques I know for moving past intentional delay. It works like this.

- Identify the project or task you have effectively shelved through procrastination.
- Set a timer, watch or alarm clock to go off in ten minutes.
- Work like crazy on the project or task until the timer rings.
- When the alarm sounds, you have permission to stop.

Chances are you won't want to stop because you will have become involved in the task. The problem with procrastinators is not doing the thing you need to do; it's getting started! Once you start, momentum keeps you going.

If, when the alarm rings, you really want to stop — stop! And stop guilt free. That's the whole point of this activity. You contracted with yourself to be able to stop after ten minutes, so honor your commitment. Walk away from the project or task, and come back later for another Ten Minute Jump Start. If nothing else, you'll eventually complete it through a series of ten minute intervals.

A TOUGH LESSON ABOUT PROCRASTINATION

I learned about procrastination the hard way. One of the things I enjoy doing is making cards for friends and family. But I wasn't good about getting the cards off in a timely way. Typically I procrastinated until the event the card was celebrating was past.

I remember making a birthday card for my grandfather, who loved getting my homemade cards. Late as usual, I sent it off the day of his birthday. That night we got a telephone call, telling us that my grandfather had died suddenly. I'll never forget arriving for his funeral the same day my card arrived in the mail. If I'd sent it on time, he would have seen it.

THE R.A.F.T. TECHNIQUE

It seems as if paper has learned how to multiply itself. Have you noticed that there seems to be more paper than ever lying around in your home as well as in your office? The ability to manage the flood of paper that comes into your life needs to be a #1 priority!

Otherwise, you can drown in it — or at least waste a lot of time wading through it! This helpful tool — the RAFT technique — will help you "float" through paperwork, and strengthen your time management skills. For each piece of paper you encounter, choose one of the actions from the **RAFT** formula:

R = Redirect It! This is a devious technique, but nonetheless very effective. The point here is to get the paper off your desk or out of your home, and onto someone else's desk or into someone else's home! Be creative! Use notes such as: For your information; Please handle; Thought you'd be interested in this; Why did I get this?; etc.

A = Act on It! It has been estimated that approximately 7 hours per week is wasted just moving paper on a desk. Get rid of it the *first* time you handle it. Use my philosophy: Every time you touch a piece of paper, move it one step closer to completion.

F = File It! Don't add it to a stack to be filed. File it! This serves two purposes. It gets paper off your desk or counter *and* it familiarizes you with the files. Everyone should have a good file cabinet in their home, for bills, warranties, receipts, personal information, self development data, etc.

T = Trash It! You could probably eliminate 50% or more of the paper on your desk or in your house and never miss it. So go ahead...*make your day.* Say a fond farewell to those useless pieces of paper taking up space, and send them on to their next assignment.

Here's a keeper for you: Remember — sometimes DONE is better than PERFECT! Corollary: Sometimes perfect is more important than done. The secret is to know the difference!

ASK YOURSELF . . .

Every so often throughout the day, stop and ask yourself this critical question: AM I MAKING THE BEST USE OF MY TIME RIGHT NOW? If the answer is "YES," then continue with what you are doing. If the answer is "NO," then stop immediately. Do not pass go. Do not collect $200. Just stop, and do whatever IS the best use of your time right now!

WHY DO WE FEEL OVERWHELMED?

In 1929, the Sorbonne Library in Paris housed 1,338 books, most handwritten, representing nearly all of humankind's accumulated knowledge spanning a few thousand years. In 1992, worldwide, over 365,000 books were published — more than 1,000 a day.

One edition of the Sunday New York Times contains more information items than the typical adult in 1892 was exposed to during an entire lifetime.

More books and articles are published in one day than you could comfortably read in the rest of your life. (from *Breathing Space: Living & Working at a Comfortable Pace in a Sped-Up Society*, Jeff Davidson)

SIMPLIFY!

We make things much too difficult for ourselves. Make it a practice as you begin to do something to stop and ask yourself this question: How can I make this easier? Become a master in the art of simplifying! For example, when you invite friends over for dinner, cook a one-dish casserole instead of a three-course meal; hand-write a note instead of typing it; buy clothes that need no ironing; throw away junk mail without opening it; keep your tools in one location — preferably on hooks for easy capture; let other people help you; get a hairstyle that is easy to maintain. Make it a game. Keep asking, how can I make this easier? How can I simplify?

CONSTRUCT A PROCRASTINATION PROFILE

Procrastination is a deadly habit, but it can be managed. The first step is to identify your "Procrastination Patterns." If you're like most people, you have one or two specific types of things you procrastinate on. And, if you're like most people, you also have one activity you do as a substitute for the thing you are avoiding. It becomes a pattern. Once the pattern is identified, you can attack and overcome it!

I'm asking you to be brutally honest with yourself. Until you recognize your delay tactics, you can't modify or eliminate non-productive behavior. So get rid of all the facades and excuses. Take a good hard look at your procrastination profile.

Use the following guide to profile yourself:

1. **What type of project(s)/situation(s) do you consistently procrastinate on** (ie, paying bills; balancing the checkbook; making telephone calls; dealing with a specific person; exercise; etc.)? If you have difficulty with this question, observe your habits for a week or two. Become acutely aware of when you are avoiding something, and write it down. Then, review the list. You'll find a pattern...I promise!

2. **Now that you're aware of** *what* **you procrastinate on, become aware of** *what you do instead.* Chances are you're doing some low-priority task to avoid the big one…and chances are you've convinced yourself that what you're doing is important. We're great at rationalizing our behavior…but remember that the word "rationalize" means just that… "rational lies!" Identify your cover-up techniques. Again, there will probably be a pattern. Examples I've seen (and experienced, I must admit) include: getting coffee (or other diversionary eating strategies); cleaning up desk, kitchen, etc; making nonessential phone calls; taking two-hour lunches; reviewing client files; rewriting material; attending unnecessary meetings (or calling them); photocopying reports (or cartoons); and the list goes on and on. In and of themselves, there is nothing wrong with any of these activities. In fact, most of them are very necessary — at the appropriate time. The question is: What #1 priority are you avoiding by performing this activity? Again, you'll begin to see a pattern.

3. **Finally, ask yourself what rewards you can establish to motivate yourself to action.** The value of the reward can range from a star on your calendar to an afternoon on the golf course or tennis court. The only condition is that the reward must be totally and completely in your control to give to yourself. I've found it most effective to match the value of the reward with the degree of avoidance you are experiencing.

If you want to make an easy job seem mighty hard, just keep putting off doing it.

(Olin Miller)

CLIP AND SAVE

Do you find yourself buried under a mountain of magazines and professional journals? You know you need to read them. You recognize they're packed with important industry-specific information or interesting stories, recipes and reports. You want to read them — someday. The very prospect seems overwhelming. They just continue to stack up, and sit there staring at you, creating feelings of guilt every time you see them.

This simple Clip and Save technique has many benefits. It will help you reduce Mt. Everest to a foothill. It will help keep you up-to-date on your reading. And it will provide you with a more productive use of "waiting time" (that dead time that is wasted when you are waiting for meetings to begin or for someone to arrive, etc.)

Retrieve a file folder, stapler, scissors and a pen. Across the tab on the file folder, write: READING FILE. Open that first journal or magazine and scan the index. Identify the articles of primary interest to you. Then clip those articles. (Hint: Be sure to get the entire article. Some articles are parceled out, with the last few paragraphs on obscure pages near the back.) Staple the articles together and place them in the *Reading File* you just created. Discard the rest of the magazine! Get in the *clip and save* habit as soon as your magazines and journals arrive. Don't give them a chance to pile up.

Whenever you travel, there will always be "down time," so slip your *Reading File* (or a few articles from it) into your attaché case. You'll never feel frustrated with wasted time again, and you'll stay current with the latest information from your journals and magazines.

Once you've read the article, make a decision to pass it on to someone else, file it or toss it. If you decide to file it, **be sure** it's reference material you really need to keep. I challenge you to avoid saving articles "just in

case you'll need to refer to them someday..." If there
are 2 or 3 key points you find useful, record them on a 3
x 5 card or log them in your computer and then toss or
re-route the article.

Remember: No one ever said, on their death bed, "I wish
I had spent more time working."

DO WHAT YOU HATE FIRST

Have you ever noticed how you procrastinate doing
the things you dislike most? What a useless thing to do!
Even when you're doing things you enjoy, the thought of
that thing you hate is lurking in the background, sabotaging any fun you could be having on the job. The way
to avoid this problem is to recognize what it is you hate
most, and do it first. That's right — do it first and get it
over with. The sense of relief you'll feel will flood
through you, bringing with it a surge of energy and satisfaction that will last the rest of the day.

When you die, they are not going to surround your
casket, look at you and say, "WOW! She sure had a
clean oven."

HOW I MADE EXERCISE A HABIT

One of things I really dislike doing is exercise.
However, because I really do enjoy eating . . . and
because my job requires an incredible amount of stami-
na . . . I had to find a way to build exercise into my
lifestyle. I tried all kinds of things. For example, I joined
a local spa. The membership card looked great in my
billfold! A friend finally suggested to me that I should
join the Y — it was cheaper to *not go to* than the Spa!

Then I decided I would join my neighbors in a daily jog around our cul-de-sac. I bought a beautiful purple jogging suit. I looked good! But on my first day of jogging around the circle, I developed a knee problem. (Let me mention here that the knee problem disappeared as soon as I stopped jogging! I believe it was a mental attitude problem, not a knee problem!).

The only thing that worked for me was to find a way to exercise first thing in the morning, before I was awake enough to change my mind! I worked with a personal trainer to develop a routine that I could do in my bedroom, using only small hand weights. It takes about 20 minutes, and I do it *every* morning. Then I feel smug all day because I know I've done my exercise for the day! For me, doing what I hate first was the secret I needed to make exercise a habit for me.

 Why is it that the things we give up first in doing too much are the things that mean the most to us, like our health, our creativity, our families, our friends, and ourselves?
(from Collect Your Thoughts Calendar)

GET OFF MAILING LISTS

Are you tired of all the junk mail that piles up on your counter or in your In-Basket? It is possible to get off some of those mailing lists by sending a request to be removed to: Direct Marketing Association, P.O. Box 9008, Farmingdale, NY 11735. Include all variations of your name.

OPEN YOUR MAIL OVER THE TRASH CAN

One of the biggest sources of clutter in my life is piled up mail that sits on my kitchen counter or covers my desk. A secret to cutting through this mess is to open the mail right over a trash can! Toss anything that is junk; file bills in a tickle file to be paid at the appropriate time; put correspondence to be answered in a special file folder designated for that purpose. Have a spot for everything, and get it there at the time you open the mail. The principle is: When you've finished going through the mail, you should not be able to tell it ever came!

Life is a checkerboard, and the player opposite you is time. *If you hesitate before moving, or neglect to move* *promptly, your markers will be wiped off the board by* *time. You are playing against a partner who will not tol-* *erate indecision.*

(Napoleon Hill)

WHAT DO YOU VALUE?

Show me your checkbook stubs and your calendar, and I will tell you what you really value!

MESSAGE NOTEBOOK

Do you have fifty-million little pieces of paper floating around with individual messages on them? If so, you understand the frustration of having messages fall through the cracks (figuratively *and* literally). I have found a solution that eliminates this problem. I keep a spiral notebook right by my telephone. Each morning I write the date at the top of the page. Notes from any telephone calls I receive are recorded in that notebook; messages from my answering service get captured there; messages others take for me get stapled right in the notebook. I draw a square by the items that need an action by me, and check it off when I complete it. It is simple to quickly scan through my notebook and identify open squares indicating actions I haven't taken yet. And these notebooks have saved me several times when I've needed to recall a person's name or telephone number.

IF I COULD JUST GET ORGANIZED

There may be nothing wrong with you —
the way you live, the work you do;

But I can very plainly see
exactly what is wrong with me.

It isn't that I'm indolent — or dodging duty by intent;
I work as hard as anyone and yet I get so little done.

The morning goes, the noon is here;
Before I know the night is near,

And all around me, I regret,
are things I haven't finished yet.

With you, there may be nothing wrong —
But here's my trouble right along,

I do the things that don't amount
to very much, of no account,

That really seem important, though;
and let a lot of matters go.

I nibble this, I nibble that, But never finish what I'm at.
I work as hard as anyone and yet I get so little done.

I'd do so much — you'd be surprised —
If I could just get organized!

(Frank Bettger)

WE'VE GOT TO STOP
MEETING LIKE THIS!

One of the biggest time robbers we experience is time spent in ineffective meetings. Whether it's meetings connected with work, professional organizations or volunteer activities, meetings eat away huge chunks of our time. Here is a quick tip list to help you make your meetings valuable, productive and fast!

- Have a specific purpose or desired outcome for the meeting. No purpose — no meeting!
- Develop an agenda, with time frames for each agenda item. Include a specific start and end time for the meeting.
- Start and end meetings on time, regardless of who's there.
- Use a Meeting Facilitator, who's only function is to keep the group on track and on time in accordance with the agenda, and to focus on the process issues of the meeting.
- Develop Key Operating Principles, post them, and review them before the meeting. Then honor them! (See the sample of Key Operating Procedures following this segment.)
- Use the Parking Lot to avoid irrelevant issues being discussed. The Parking Lot is a sheet of chart paper posted on the wall; whenever an issue not on the agenda comes up, it gets listed on that page so it won't be forgotten. It is either addressed at the end of the meeting if there is time, becomes part of the agenda for the next meeting or is assigned to someone for action.
- Use gimmicks to help keep people focused on the Key Operating Principles. For example, I put a koosh ball in the center of the table. Anyone who catches someone violating one of our Key Operating Principles has permission to throw the koosh at that person! I also designed a special sign of a dead horse, inside one of those circles with a slash through it, signifying "No Dead Horses." When anyone feels an issue has reached the Dead Horse stage, all they need to do is pick up that sign and wave it.
- Incorporate Group Memory in place of more traditional minutes. Group Memory is done by capturing key comments, ideas and decisions on chart paper and posting it around the room. Late-comers can catch up

just by reading the wall. This also keeps the meeting moving; if someone repeats something, you can simply refer to the wall to remind them it's been covered.

- When you are invited to a meeting, ask the question: What is my role? Why do I need to attend? You'd be amazed how often people are invited to meetings to avoid hurt feelings, when there is no real need to even be there!

- Post all commitments and decision points on chart paper for everyone to see. This avoids misunderstandings. When appropriate, be certain there is a responsible individual identified for every action, along with a date.

- Summarize key points at the end of the meeting.

SAMPLE OF KEY OPERATING PROCEDURES FOR MEETINGS

- Start and end meetings on time.
- Stick to the agenda; defer side issues to the Parking Lot.
- Come prepared and participate fully.
- Treat each other with respect.
- Welcome differing ideas.
- Bury dead horses.
- One person talks at a time; listen with the intent to understand.
- Honor commitments.

VISUAL PROP SAVES MEETING TIME

One of my clients used an interesting technique to cut their meeting time dramatically. The manager took each staff member's salary, and determined the salary-related cost per minute of the meeting. Then he posted the total cost, just in terms of salaries, and wrote it in large black numbers at each 5-minute interval on a large wall clock. His meetings became very short and productive!

THE LEGEND OF EATING
THE ELEPHANT

An old fable tells about a group of cavemen who came upon an elephant, lying dead on the side of a trail. The men had been hunting for several days, unsuccessfully, and were thrilled to have the elephant more or less handed to them on a silver platter. All they had to do was figure out how to eat it.

One of the men sketched a diagram in the dirt of a huge rotisserie-type affair, designed to roast the elephant. Another tried to figure out how large a pot would be needed to boil the elephant.

A third hungry caveman suggested throwing the elephant onto a huge bonfire. None of the ideas seemed practical or feasible, and the cavemen became more and more frustrated. Finally, the smallest and youngest of the cavemen tentatively indicated he had a suggestion. The others snickered, but decided to let the little guy have his say.

Shyly but confidently, the youngest of the cavemen said, "Here's my suggestion. Why don't we eat this elephant one bite at a time?"

• • • • • • • •

This fable has a message concerning the management of time. If we try to completely overhaul our daily practices, changing everything at once, we will become hopelessly confused and frustrated. Even worse, we will probably feel under more time pressure, rather than less.

The secret to effective management of time is sort of like eating that elephant — you have to do it "one bite at a time!" Choose one thing and focus on it until it becomes a habit; then work on something else. Bit by bit, you will begin to see a real change in your life, as you manage your time by eating the elephant, one bite at a time.

ply ask: "How do you suggest we resolve this?"
Pretty soon people will stop coming in with problems to dump on you!

Of course, it goes without saying [but I'm going to say it anyway!] that if your job is problem solving, this may not be the technique you want to use!

If you don't know you have it or where to find it, it's of no use to you.

(Barbara Hemphill)

A HAT TRICK

Put on your hat or coat the moment there's a knock at your door. If it's someone you want to see, say you just came in. If it's someone you don't want to spend time with, say you're on your way out.

A 'BRIEFCASE' STUDY

The story is told of a man who carried his overstuffed briefcase home from work each night, then spent hours in his study after dinner on things brought from the office. His little daughter was confused, and asked her mother: "Why doesn't daddy have time to play with me any more?"

Her mother explained: "Daddy has a new job now, with lots of responsibility. He can't get all his work finished so he has to bring some of it home to work on after supper."

The little girl looked at her mother sadly, then brightened as she got an idea. "I know," she exclaimed. "Why don't we see if they can move daddy to a slower class?"

Showing a tour group around a museum, the guide said, "That fossil in the glass case is two million and nine years old."

"How can you date it so precisely?" someone asked admiringly.

"That's easy," replied the guide. "I've been working here nine years, and it was two million years old when I came."

(From the *Financial Times*, London)

Remember — time flies, but you are the pilot!

LIFE'S DANCE

Life stretches before me like a giant dance floor.
I step out, never knowing what music I will hear.
Some days I'm able to flow through life,
     gently rising and falling in a spectacular waltz.
Other days are more like a swing,
     where I'm triple-stepping to stay in tune —
     changing direction, whirling this way and that.
The joy of Life's Gigantic Ballroom is the partnership of the
     dance —
For I know I'm not out there alone.
In my partner I have a chemistry that transcends the steps of
     the dance.
Together we can move in the same direction, changing rhythms
     with the music, matching steps and keeping time
And even stepping "outside the lines" to improvise and stretch
     ourselves.
When we turn apart to perform some intricate pattern on our own
We are secure in knowing that we will always return to the safe
     haven of a solid dance position.

Sure, we may miss some steps here and there — and occasionally
     land on each other's toes —
But if we never made mistakes, we'd never learn to perform
     the dance.
And through the missteps we learn the art of recovery . . . of helping
     each other move gently back into the rhythm of Life . . .
Never looking down — always with a smile.

And even with my partner, there are times we find we are expected
to do a dance we've not yet learned.
That's when we discover that out there on Life's dance floor there
*   are teachers who will show us the patterns, demonstrate*
*   the flowing movement, and provide a strong lead —*
If only we can learn how to follow.
They gently guide us through the unknown and give the gift of
*   new skills — then quietly move away*
So we can joyfully navigate the patterns when we meet this dance
*   again.*

As I enter Life's Ballroom and greet my partner,
*   May I listen for the music —*
And whether it's a waltz or a rumba, a cha-cha or a swing,
*   a tango or a fox-trot — or some dance I've yet to learn —*
May I listen for the rhythm and adjust my movements,
And may I always be in touch with my Cosmic Teachers who
*   will guide me.*
May I learn when to lead and when to follow so I will always be
*   flowing in time with the music*
And dancing through Life with joy.

(Cher Holton)

BRINGING HARMONY TO LIFE

Do you feel frazzled and out of control?
Are conflicting priorities taking their toll?
Are you up-tight, burned out, filled with anxiety?
Are you ready for changes? Do you want HARMONY?

Stop blaming the past for what's wrong with you;
Don't let circumstances define what you do;
When you're locked in by fear, overwhelmed hopelessly --
Put your life back in focus -- you can have HARMONY.

You make the choices each moment - each day;
You choose your reactions, your thoughts, what you say;
You can write your own script - choose your cast carefully --
And with you as director you will have HARMONY!

CHORUS: Harmony -- Harmony
*   That's how life's supposed to be.*
*   Feeling peaceful -- Feeling fit*
*   In control and loving it!*
*   Achieving goals and having fun*
*   Body, Mind and Soul are one.*
*   My intuition says it's right --*
*   Bringing harmony to life.*

(Cher Holton)

MEET THE AUTHOR

Cher Holton, President and co-founder of The Holton Consulting Group, Inc., is a Corporate Impact Consultant focusing on the Human Side of Quality. Known for her unique Turbo-Training™ and Retreat Forward™ Team Development concepts, Cher serves a diverse clientele of corporate, government and healthcare organizations. She is uniquely able to blend her skills as speaker, trainer, consultant and group facilitator to provide dynamic, customized, practical programs for her clients around the country.

Cher is one of less than two dozen professionals world-wide who have earned both the Certified Speaking Professional and the Certified Management Consultant designations. She possesses a Ph.D. focusing in Human Resource Development, is past President of the Carolinas Chapter of National Speakers Association, is active in several professional and civic organizations, and is recipient of the Flawless Consulting Medallion.

On a personal note, Cher and her husband Bil (yes, that's Bil with one "L") take what they call Indiana Jones Experiences, including white-water rafting, sky-diving, and even fire-walking! Cher enjoys mystery and spy novels, the theatre, and bears (she has a huge collection]! She is a member of the United States Amateur Ballroom Dance Association, and competes with Bil as an Amateur Student Couple. They have won national awards in several dances.

For information about bringing Cher to your organization or association, please contact her through:

The Holton Consulting Group, Inc.
1405 Autumn Ridge Drive, Durham. NC 27712
877.819.7489 • 919.767.9620 • Fax 866.500.7697
www.holtonconsulting.com • cher@holtonconsulting.com

INDEX